RECEIVE

שלום

Receive Fullness of Life Through Christ

Revision:
Scribe Marketer Team

Editorial Production:
Vancler Santos

Cover Art:
Scribe Marketer Team

Layout:
Vancler Santos

Scribe Marketer Ltda.
445 Broad Hollow Rd
Melville, NY 11747
(215) 336-5094
contact@scribenet.com
www.scribemarketer.com

Publication and Cataloging Data

ISBN: 979-8-89587-514-8
Vancler Santos

RECEIVE שָׁלוֹם Shalom
Receive Fullness of Life Through Christ
Staten House; 2024; 176p.

Spirituality; Education

Staten House

RECEIVE

שלום

Receive Fullness of Life Through Christ

Vancler Santos

1st Edition | 2024

New York | USA

Foreword

My intention was never to write a book but rather a testimony of how God, in the 21st century, continues to intervene in His creation to change the fortune of those who seek Him. Though I am not worthy of His favor, our Creator still cares for the little ones and, to the glory of His Name, bestows life, vigor, and success upon His beloved.

As I wrote my personal story, the Spirit of the Lord helped me understand the reason for all that I have experienced and the precious lessons I have learned as I have passed through the fire. One of the greatest principles I have learned is that a good life requires balance and that spiritual things are manifested on Earth. Jesus said that whoever would seek first the Kingdom of God, and its righteousness would receive all other things (as stated in Matthew 6:33). We can easily misinterpret this verse by thinking that we should only pursue spiritual things, and the result will be success in all other areas without struggle, but that is not what the Messiah said nor meant. As our example, He acted in the earthly sphere with the same intensity and passion as in spiritual matters. He said to seek first the Kingdom, not to seek only the Kingdom of God. Nor did He say that if we seek the Kingdom, the rest of the things would fall into our laps from heaven, but rather that they would be added to our lives. If we read the verse in its context, we can also see that He was speaking of our basic needs, such as clothing, food, and shelter, in addition to physical conditions that every human being desires, needs, and seeks to achieve. These include health, love, family, financial security, prosperity, and peace. He promised that these thingswould be added and not given. Thus, we must always do our part and strive to obtain these blessings while seeking first the Kingdom and the will of God if we are to succeed.

Through a tragedy in my life, the Almighty rescued me, restored me, and taught me lessons I would never have learned otherwise. Now, on the other side of the battle, I have a heart full of grace and a thousandfold love for the gift of life and the Life-Giver. I hope my story can inspire you to get to know Him more intimately and make a difference in your life in a practical way.

These lessons taught me that not everything is spiritual and that even our Messiah was a man on Earth. He went through the same struggles, temptations, hardships, and problems that we go through, but in all of them, He was more than a conqueror. The life of Jesus was an example that we should emulate as best we can. He loved the Father with all His heart (desires, intentions, and mind), soul (breath and life), and strength (deeds and works). He obeyed the commandments and teachings of the Father in every detail. He sought, prayed, fasted, studied the Scriptures, and applied them to His life. But He also worked, had a profession, cared for his health, and performed everyday tasks that the Bible does not mention. I'm sure He brushed His teeth, bathed, washed dishes, helped His mother with household chores, played as a child with His little friends, got sick, made jokes, danced, laughed, cried, and all the other things that are human experiences. Sometimes, it's easy to forget that this was God's plan from the beginning... that God, the Creator of all things, visible and invisible, came into the world to dwell among us and teach us how to attain wholeness and fullness of life. What an inexplicable and incomprehensible love! The love of our Father, whose greatest desire is to gift His creation with His שָׁלוֹם Shalom[1] and love.

---

1 שָׁלוֹם Shalom, in Hebrew, means much more than peace. The best translation would be "completeness" or "fullness."

To the Reader

Thank you in advance for your attention in reading this book. You will find on the following pages many testimonies of miraculous works that God has performed in my life over the past six years, but also several practical lessons that I have applied to obtain these victories.

God can do everything, but He specializes in performing miracles and doesn't do what we're supposed to do. Therefore, in writing this book, I focused on the behaviors that can be applied in your life and transform your destiny as well. Knowing that each reader will be at a different stage of life, I have spared no details in the examples and instructions. I hope that each of you can learn at least one good lesson that inspires you to change and draw closer to the Creator.

Speaking of practical lessons, you may have received this book for free. My intention is to publish and print this book and give it as a gift to as many people as possible. I invested time, love, affection, and money to make this a reality. If you are blessed by this book or touched by the Holy Spirit to give an offering or bless others with the same generosity, I humbly accept your participation. Becoming a partner in this vision He has given me will be an investment in the Kingdom of God. The money raised will be used exclusively to publish more copies and pass on the blessing to others who may not be in the same position to obtain the book if any monetary value is required, however small.

Contact me via Instagram or Facebook or give the offering to the person distributing the book. You may also give on the internet, through the website:

www.think-like-jesus.com/support

Dedication

I dedicate this book to my dear wife, Susan Santos, and my wonderful daughter, Isabella. They inspired me and were used by God to awaken within me the desire to love them as He commands. Love is not based on feelings but rather on action. It cannot be expressed without sacrifice. True love surpasses all things and always seeks the well-being of others. When I was at the end of my strength, God reminded me that there are people who are always by my side and that now it was my turn to fight for them. Just as Christ loved the Church unto death, He taught me that I should love my family in the same way. Love for my family was the catalyst the Holy Spirit used to help me overcome and conquer the giants that lay ahead of me.

I also dedicate it to my mother, Vânia Moreira, and my sister, Cynthia Barbosa. Two spiritual warriors who have added so much to my life in the last six years. And to Pastor Tânia Tereza, who was the channel of blessing that God used to heal my body and soul. Pastor Tânia's ministry specializes in healing and deliverance and has touched thousands of lives across the world by putting the Lord's Word into practice.

Every change that has manifested in my life since my healing has been from the desire to do my best for them and to honor my Heavenly Father for the new opportunity to live a life worthy of his love.

Table of Contents

1. Root of the Problem

When we face an obstacle or problem, our first reaction is to look for the quickest possible solution. If our focus is too spiritual, we tend to start praying incessantly and not take any action. If it is carnal, we will try to find a way to solve the problem, and only after we do not see results, we will say a quick prayer. But I've learned that both extremes are incorrect. Before successfully finding any solution, we must understand the root of the problem. Nowadays, most people treat the symptoms to bring temporary relief but fail to see the root cause, thus failing to find a real solution.

Of course, as followers of Christ, the best thing to do is to seek God and pray, but if we stop there, we probably won't be able to solve anything. No wonder so many believers are living in defeat. Ask God for wisdom and discernment because not everything is spiritual. In contrast, don't try to use God as your personal ATM. Only seeking Him when you need to make a withdrawal to meet a need or personal desire. We must instead ask God for strategy and His blessing as we act. Understand that God specializes in working miracles and accomplishing the impossible. This means that if something is possible and within your reach, He probably won't do it for you.

I have never forgotten a seminary class I took when I was a recent convert. The teacher of the class was Pastor Álvaro Cruz, and he made an illustration that revolutionized my way of thinking. He was the first to use the phrase "not everything is spiritual," at least in my life. His statement was followed by an illustration. I don't know if this story was meant as a parable or if it was based on real events. It's irrelevant because the lesson demonstrated by it was simply brilliant. He narrated

11

the following story to the class:

A church member approached me with a serious financial problem and said:

— "Pastor, I'm in serious debt. This debt has been growing for many years, and now it has become out of control."

I responded by saying that God would help. Then I said a fervent prayer with him.

After the prayer, I counseled him as follows:

— "Start by making a spreadsheet with your monthly income and all your expenses. A budget reflecting your current condition. Then ask God to give you a strategy and a solution to get out of that debt."

A few months later, I met with this man again and asked him how the situation progressed.

— "Nothing has changed, pastor," he lamented. "In fact, things got worse."

— "Did you make the spreadsheet as I had instructed?" I asked. "Can I take a look to give you suggestions?" I added.

— "I haven't had time to make the spreadsheet yet, pastor, but I'll do it, and then I'll share it to get your..."

— "You don't have to. I already know what your problem is." I abruptly interrupted him mid-sentence.

The gentleman looked at me with shock but new hope and shouted:

— "Glory to God!" After a brief pause, he added with enthusiasm, "Let's rebuke the devourer and get the victory."

I called him into my office and asked him to take all the credit cards out of his wallet and place them on my desk. He quickly complied, thinking that I would probably pray over them. Maybe anoint them or do something spiritual and mystical. However, the gentleman almost had a heart attack when I, instead of doing what he expected, cut all the credit cards with scissors. Furious, he yelled:

— "Pastor, are you crazy? Why did you do that?"

— "I've come to the conclusion that what you really needed was plastic surgery," I replied with a smirk while keeping my voice low in a sarcastic tone. "Your problem is not spiritual. What you need to do is have discipline, stop using these credit cards as a crutch, and take back control of your financial life. You've asked me for help, and I'm giving you my opinion and direction from God. Now, the next step is yours. You can call the banks and easily get new cards issued and sent to you, or you can use this opportunity to make that spreadsheet, track your expenses, and pay off the debt. The second option is more difficult, but with God's help, you will receive victory. Decide what you want to do, and if you need

13

me, I'll continue to help you."

The pastor didn't even reveal to the class the outcome of this story, but that was not his purpose to begin with. The truth is that he wanted to convey, by means of this illustration, was "not everything is spiritual." Sometimes, as Christians, we lose all sense of reality. When we try to deal with physical problems only in the spiritual realm, we rarely succeed. In the same way, when the problem is spiritual, nothing in the physical realm will solve it. Therefore, before finding the solution to any dilemma, we first need to identify the root of the problem.

2. Revelations

There are moments in our lives that can only be described as divine revelations. They are those in which, in the blink of an eye, we come to understand profound truths, and there is no explanation of how these revelations occurred.

One of those periods, for me, was on May 26, 2010, at 2:52 p.m., when I became a dad. I gasped as I admired the miracle that had just happened before my eyes. My heart was almost bursting with excitement, and suddenly, one of those revelations materialized: "I am now responsible for another human being." It was the most beautiful and terrifying event of my life. That same day, I prayed one of the sincerest prayers. Filled with fear and love, I uttered these words:

— "Father, please grant me wisdom and strength to raise my daughter in Your ways. Help me to be the best father I can be and to be a living Bible for her. May Jesus be the most important person in her life. Amen."

There aren't many life-defining moments, but when my daughter's little hand wrapped itself around my finger, my reality shifted, and I surrendered my life for the third time. The first was in the summer of 1992, as soon as I understood that I needed a Savior; The second was when I said "I do" to my soulmate on June 24, 2005; And the third was that day when I learned that my life had been extended beyond my own body through my daughter's eyes.

Up until that time, I was a typical young man without any concern about the details of life. I just lived in the moment. I was a hard worker, but I didn't truly worry about the future. If the bills were being paid and I had the money to do what I wanted, I felt that everything was grand. I did not realize how privileged I was and how I was blessed with health, financial provision, and a beautiful family. Like I said, I was a typical guy.

In an instant, as I looked at that innocent child in my arms — a true marvel, utterly fragile and dependent on others for everything — I was horrified by the worries that flooded my mind. My immediate desire was to give her the world. The best clothes, food, home, medical insurance, education, and everything else that even I didn't get to have at her age. As I continued to ponder, I began to recognize what was more important. It just turns out that they were mostly non-material. My daughter would need affection, love, and many emotional needs met. I would have to help her feel accepted, valued, and understood. Adding to those would be her spiritual needs. This meant that I would need to protect her from the negative influence of this world as well as shelter her from the enemy of our souls.

As much as I wanted to do all this, I understood at that moment that I was flawed and could never be there all the time. I quickly realized that the only way to succeed as a parent was to depend on and trust the Almighty. This meant fuller dedication to the Lord or knowing that I would face certain failure in that mission.

That is when the Spirit reminded me once again that all these thoughts and things were important and relevant. However, if I were not present in her life, it would all be in vain. If I loved her only with words and didn't physically struggle to provide the necessary physical things, she would never understand the love I so desperately wanted her to know and experience. No matter how noble my intentions were.

All these thoughts reminded me of the following passages in the letter from James:

"Suppose a brother or a sister is without clothes and daily food. If one of you says to them, 'Go in peace; keep warm and well fed,' but does nothing about their physical needs, what good is it? In the same way, faith by itself, if it is not accompanied by action, is dead." James 2:15-17 (NIV)

These passages were never so clear to me as they were at that moment. Love always requires action and self-sacrifice. The revelation was unmistakable: If we only pay lip service to love, then our love is not real.

3. Body, Soul, and Spirit

I recall one of my many conversations with an atheist where he asked me the following question:

— "How do you explain that the Bible says that God is only One, but you believers in Christ say that there is the Father, the Son, and the Holy Spirit, but that all three are God?"

The most intellectually honest answer I could give him was this:

— "No one really knows. This is a real mystery, and our limited minds cannot fully come close to grasping it."

This is such a phenomenon that we have invented a doctrine and name to describe it: the Trinity.

The word "Trinity" is not even in the Holy Scriptures. It's one of those religious terms we've come up with to explain what we don't understand, like "rapture." Even "Bible" is a religious term, for it comes from the Greek "βιβλία," which simply means "books."

But just because no one understands the phenomenon doesn't mean it's not accurate or real. Ask any theoretical scientist or professor of Theoretical Mathematics, and I guarantee you they will agree with me. Did you know that, to this day, science does not know how to explain certain forces, such as gravity? But that's not to say that force doesn't exist, right? Everyone can feel the gravitational force and see its effect. Just jump off a building and, believing it or not, understanding it or not, you'll certainly fall. Obviously, I'm not encouraging this because, depending on the height, you will get hurt or die. Still, I think the point stands.

The same is true with Quantum Physics. Did you know that, according to science, no one knows the exact location of quantum particles? And that two entangled particles react immediately, no matter how far apart they are? And that, in the physical world, we cannot see anything beyond the fourth dimension, but that, in Higher Mathematics, science has already found at least ten dimensions that describe reality?

What's my point? There are more questions that we don't understand or can't explain than there are questions that have ready answers. In cosmology, we are only able to account for 4% of everything that can be calculated in our observed gravitational pull. Black holes, dark matter, and many other things added to fill the gaps exist only in theory, but they are part of reality.

I often tell my daughter the following:

— "Growing in knowledge is not the same as growing in wisdom. Knowledge is getting information, but wisdom is applying knowledge in the right way."

For example, if you are taught that smoking causes lung cancer and is addictive, you have been given knowledge. These are just facts that you may not have known before. To persist in the activity after learning about its consequences is equated to using the information foolishly. If you decide to quit, then you have chosen to use the information wisely.

I continue the lesson by telling her that there is a massive difference between being foolish and ignorant. Many are offended by the word "ignorant," but we are all ignorant in some areas. Being ignorant is not an insult. It simply means that we don't know something. In the area of crochet, for example, I'm 100% ignorant. Using the same example, if you smoke all your life without having received the information about cancer, you are not being foolish, just ignorant. Of course, both are not desirable, but only one of them makes you morally responsible. As children of God, we are encouraged to seek both knowledge and wisdom.

"My people have been destroyed from lack of knowledge." Hosea 4:6 (NIV)

"If any of you lacks wisdom, you should ask God, who gives generously to all without finding fault, and it will be given to you." James 1:5 (NIV)

Solomon's proverbs add further revelation about wisdom. In Proverbs 9:10, he states that fear is the beginning of wisdom. Makes us wonder. Why "fear?" It's actually quite simple and logical to understand. Fear of judgment or negative consequences for our mistakes leads us to do what is right before God and others. Fear, in general, leads us to make good decisions. As we have illustrated with the knowledge of smoking and its consequences, people who fear getting sick or even dying will probably do anything to quit smoking. It is unfortunate that for many, without fear, there is little incentive to put the effort to do what is right or good. Nevertheless, it seems like the standard for human nature.

I apologize for going on a tangent. Let's return to the subject of the enigmatic Trinity. Even though we do not have the full knowledge of how God can be One and Three at the same time, we can see examples that help us understand. Not explain or define it, but understand it to a degree. In fact, our very nature can be a way of demonstrating this. Even if this insight is foreign to us, we acknowledge that we are body, soul, and spirit (most of us, anyway). In a way, we are also a "trinity." We have a physical body, which is used to interact with everything around us; a soul, which gives us access to emotions and feelings and is connected to our mind, which controls our body; and a spirit, which gives us access to the spiritual realm and the ability to communicate with God.

Science and Psychology have limited knowledge about the areas of the soul and spirit. As much as we understand about our being, there is no consensus in the data and studies done in these areas. The body is the easiest to understand, as we can see it, touch it, smell it, and even taste it, but the mind and emotions are still a big mystery. We know the location of the brain, but consciousness is not located inside the organ in a palpable way. It resides in a remote place. It is like a radio that receives the frequency and manifests the voice of the singers and their instruments. Everyone understands and knows that inside the radio, there are no miniature instruments or people singing. That's how it is with the brain and mind.

The body, soul, and spirit work together, and they overlap with each other, thus forming you. The body alone is not "you." The soul alone is not "you." Spirit alone is not "you." You are the composition of the three in one person. In a way, God is like that too. Well, not exactly, but as I said, it's a way to help us better understand the concept of the Trinity and the complexity of God. If God could be explained and defined by human terms, then He would cease to be God. Consequently, we need to proceed with caution when we think we know exactly who He is and how He operates.

What lesson can we learn from all of this? If we are body, soul, and spirit, which is more important? I believe all three are equally important, and if any one of these areas is neglected, we will suffer. This suffering will reveal itself in our body because every expression of our Ego is completed in the body and physical realm. Physical illnesses can originate in the body itself, just as they can be caused by uncontrolled emotions or spiritual problems. According to what we have discussed earlier, to resolve any conflict, we must discern its root before tackling it.

Imagine, for a minute, an iceberg floating in the ocean. You can only see a small percentage of the iceberg above the waters. Normally, only 10 to 15 percent of the ice is above the horizon; the rest is below, hidden in the icy waters. It's the same with us. Our material body represents only a small percentage of our complex life and being. The subconscious, the conscious, and the emotional, psychological, and spiritual sides make up the other 85% that we can't see but can cause us real problems. Regardless of the source of the problem, it can be experienced and seen in the physical body. This is how:

Every action begins in the mind, in our thoughts. Actions become habits; Habits become our life and its fruits. What we feel gives impulse to our thoughts, and our thoughts drive everything else.

Human psychology is so complex that not even medical professionals fully understand each individual. On top of all this, each person also has outside influences. It's no wonder that being confused and morbid is the norm in most people.

The reality is that most people are ignorant of these facts — no wonder we are in the condition we are in today. But I'm thankful to God, who revealed certain things within me that changed my life. These inner reflections led me to act and transform my habits to achieve balance. And now He gives me the opportunity to share what I've learned with you. Information that you can apply to your situation or at least, it is my hope, to prompt you to explore your own ways of achieving the same. What you do with this information is up to you. Will you be wise and allow the information to influence you by applying it to your circumstances? I truly hope so.

4. Upside Down

Now that we understand that we are three distinct but interconnected parts, we can better understand why certain things happen in certain ways. Or, at the very least, to have an instrument to help give a more effective diagnosis when we face problems. However, before moving forward, it is important to understand that some areas of our being cannot be reached directly. How so? I'll give you an example to make it easier to visualize this concept.

Let's suppose you're examining your life, and you conclude that the problem you're facing is emotional and that its consequence is attacking your physical body. Even if your habits are being affected by your emotions, the resolution of the problem will only take place through the physical. This is where reality is manifested, and the beginning of the solution will be revealed. Understand that I'm not giving medical advice here. I don't have a degree in medicine or psychology. In fact, I suffered from depression that was solved through the help of a psychologist and drug administration. Still, I had to recognize the root cause, and then I had to act. The moment I understood that my emotional state was shaken, I needed to address it, knowing that I could only resolve this through the physical realm by acting. If I had not acted by seeking professionals, I would have stayed the same or probably gotten worse.

I'll restate this because it is important: emotions drive thoughts, thoughts direct actions, actions become habits, and these become our life and its fruits.

There is a Russian scientist who has done research in the psychological field to prove this statement. His name was

Pavlov, and his most famous experiment was with the study of dogs and their behavior. Through those experiments, he conclusively showed that our feelings affect our actions. That our brains can be conditioned to act in a programmed way.

During these experiments, Pavlov would ring a bell and throw a piece of meat at the dog being observed. He did this hundreds of times with several dogs over several weeks. When the animals' behavior became a habit, he began to ring the bell without throwing the meat and realized that the animals became conditioned to act in a certain way. He noted that their mouths would immediately salivate in anticipation of receiving the piece of meat, even if the meat was not present.

In a sense, our feelings are equivalent to the bell in this research. When we receive immediate pleasure from some activity, we begin to associate the action with the pleasurable outcome. Today's social platforms were created with this concept to get us hooked. When we receive a "like" or a positive comment, our brain and glands in our body release hormones that give us pleasure. Dopamine rushes through our veins, causing euphoria and giving us a sense of immediate contentment. Science proves that this neurotransmitter is equivalent to and has the same effects as heroin, one of the most addictive drugs in existence. Creators of social networks talk about this topic openly, and most don't let their own children use them. Many who work in this industry do what they call "dopamine fasting." A period of weeks and even months spent away from the social networks to avoid getting addicted. Yet these same people promote the platforms to the general public.

By gaining this information, we begin to understand that we are living upside down. Most of the source of our problems lies in the hidden part of the iceberg, yet we focus all our energy on the exposed part — at the tip of it.

It is a paradox. At the same time, I am saying that we have to stop paying attention only to the physical; I am saying that we can only solve problems through it. It will make more sense in the next chapters when I give more practical examples that have worked in my life. For now, I'm just laying a foundation for the concepts to make sense when fully fleshed out. I'm certain they work, as I'm living proof of that.

To reinforce your confidence that what I've learned works, in the next chapter, I'll offer a brief glimpse of how radically my life has changed after I began to apply what I've learned from the Lord and these circumstances.

5. Transformation

In 2018, I found myself completely broke financially. Unemployed, in poor health, depressed, and with no dreams, goals, or desire to improve. I could hardly get out of bed, and to be honest, I was just waiting for death. How I got to this point is a pretty long story, but the transformation that came over my life shortly after was obvious to everyone around me. Most importantly, the change was evident to me.

What caused such a radical change was a miraculous and divine intervention. I'll tell you all about it in detail in later chapters, but for now, I'll summarize.

I was the victim of a failed surgery that damaged my Vagus nerve. The nerve that connects the brain to all the vital organs of the body. The site of the damage affected my stomach and my ability to digest solid foods. Many are not aware that the stomach is a muscle and that when we eat, it makes a movement that helps digestion before the food passes into the small intestine. After a few months of suffering, I was diagnosed with a terrible disease called gastroparesis, which can cause a slow and painful death. To be more exact, the disease itself rarely leads to death, but its side effects leave the body so debilitated that most people who acquire it eventually pass away due to other health problems that are linked to it.

As if it wasn't horrible enough to suffer from a chronic illness, I also had to deal with the indifference of the people around me. I had to deal with the judgments from people who knew little about the disease. This even included the medical staff when I visited the emergency room. They insinuated that I was faking the symptoms to get drugs or gather attention. People who suffer from this condition usually do not show on the outside what they are going through on the inside. They simply look normal, which causes confusion and misunderstandings. This dynamic adds a psychological and emotional dimension, making the situation even more challenging. Rarely will one find a person suffering from this illness who is not also dealing with depression as one of its many side effects.

Over the years, the best description I can offer about gastroparesis in layman's terms is this: a person who is starving themselves at a banquet. This is because even if your favorite food is accessible to you, you can't eat it without getting sick. You fear eating it because you know there is a high chance that you will end up in the hospital or be in agonizing pain.

Side effects accumulate progressively over the years. Physical symptoms include continuous vomiting, nausea, constipation or diarrhea, poor nutrition, lack of energy, insomnia, anxiety, and excruciating chronic pain. I was diagnosed in 2011 and suffered these symptoms for eight years. With no light at the end of the tunnel, no response from the heavens, or any hope from the medical community. Perhaps, by now, you can understand why I fell into depression.

Today, I can proudly say, to the glory of God and as a testimony to His infinite power, that I am in one of the best phases of my life. Just as God did with Job, He is restoring my life and even improving it. I'm not where I want to be yet, but the transformation is undeniable.

I was cured completely and miraculously. Gastroparesis has no known cure or effective treatment, so I can say it was a miracle. That's reason enough to celebrate. But God delivers on His promises when we listen to His instructions! Ever since I began to seek His Kingdom with more intensity and integrity, He has been adding "all other things" into my life.

In the financial area, He has supplied everything I need. Over time, I was able to pay off bills that were overdue and had piled up over the years. All the medical bills that accumulated have been eliminated. I am debt-free. Everything is up to date, and I now can set my eyes on a better future. I was able to purchase the house of my dreams. And all this while, I have blessed others as never before. I've forgotten the meaning of the word "tithe," for I'm sure I give twice as much or more than I did before. It is indeed wonderful to live this verse from Acts 20, "It is more blessed to give than to receive" (verse 35). I encourage you to be a channel of God's blessings, and they will flow through you and give you unspeakable joy.

In the health department, I was so weak that a walk felt like a marathon. At 5'11" tall, I weighed only 100lbs and had lost most of the muscle mass in my entire body. Today, however, I am healthy and fit, with the ability to eat well and exercise.

Lastly, regarding my quality of life, I feel like a reborn child. I'm exploring and learning so many new things: studying Hebrew, reading various books, drawing, and even venturing into playing the piano (I still need a lot of practice... laughs). I was even able to get the coveted PMI certification in Project Management. A certification on par with a Certified Accountant. It will help me leverage my career and increase my financial prospects in the future. Let's not forget that I am also writing this book and teaching through videos on my YouTube channel.

Everything I have been doing seems impossible because of my time constraints. Because my dear wife is going through her own health challenges, I have to take on a lot of added responsibilities. I take care of the home chores, which include cleaning, laundry, and the never-ending tasks I took for granted. I also do all the grocery shopping and cooking, additionally helping my daughter with her school activities and homework. If anything, it has increased my appreciation for all my wife had to do before. I know that as we go through this current trial, God is teaching us even more, and in due time, He will heal her as he did me. As I wait on Him, I move forward with a smile on my face because His love in my life has been supernatural. God's Shalom is unfathomable. Even during troubles, we feel complete in Him. This is the Shalom I wish for you who are reading this testimony:

"Peace (Shalom) I leave with you; my peace (Shalom) I give you. I do not give to you as the world gives. Do not let your hearts be troubled and do not be afraid." John 14:27 (NIV - emphasis added)

So that you, too, may have the life that Jesus promised:

"... I have come that they may have life and have it to the full (Shalom)." John 10:10 (NIV - emphasis added)

6. Baby Steps

When I recognized I'd been healed, I became as confused as I was amazed. I had cried out to God for so long and so persistently that when I received an answer, I began to doubt it. I continually questioned whether He had really healed me.

— "It must be a temporary remission," I thought to myself.

And I had good reason because during the eight years I suffered from the disease, I had a few short periods of transient remission. They would last roughly a week, and in every instance, I thought God had healed me. However, soon after a period of relief, I had new episodes that landed me in the hospital. Every time this occurred, I would think I was healed and even stopped taking my medication "by faith." My wife would get furious at my actions because I ended up making the situation worse every time. My intentions were genuine: to honor God and demonstrate faith. I quickly learned that without God's direction, what I was doing was not pleasing to Him, nor did it work.

The lesson learned was this: If God tells you to do something, obey it, but if it's not a specific, divine commandment, it's best not to do it and to ask for confirmation.

Like a scolded cat, this time, I was prudent. Even though I felt better, I continued to take the meds. Instead of acting my way, I prayed and asked for God's direction. Gradually, I felt the Spirit's direction and response. I was convicted of the healing by His Spirit and physical evidence, not by my feelings or thoughts.

What do I mean by physical evidence? Well, a week went by, and I didn't have any episodes. I didn't have nausea, and I didn't vomit. I was even able to eat solid food without consequences. One week turned into two, and two turned into a month. By the time I reached the third month, I was completely convinced: God had healed me! I didn't understand how it had happened, but I knew God had done the impossible! Hallelujah!

Of course, I was still dealing with so many other side effects. Over the course of eight years, I was taking strong prescriptions for depression and pain. Drugs that make the body addicted and dependent. In fact, they are medications that should not even be stopped abruptly, as they can even cause death if they are not well administered. The effects of withdrawal from these drugs can cause a lot of harm. Once more, through the Lord's direction and my mother's counsel, I applied wisdom and caution moving forward. I decreased the doses of the medicine very slowly until I was free of its effects. It took more than six months to achieve this; it was truly baby steps. The healing was immediate, but the deliverance was a journey and manifested gradually.

God is not limited in His power. If He wants, He can set you free, deliver, or heal you in an instant, but if He wants, He can also do what He did in my life. In everything and in all things, He has a purpose. For me, it was the school of hard knocks. The things He taught me in the desert are lessons I will never forget.

"And we know that in all things God works for the good of those who love him, who have been called according to his purpose." Romans 8:28 (NIV)

7. What Now, Lord?

I found myself in a new territory. I was completely healed, with a new lease on life, but everything was a disaster.

— "What now, Lord?" I thought.

I felt as if a great injustice had happened. It wasn't my fault that I got sick and that everything went down this spiral. I was free of that heinous disease, but my life was still in shambles. So much clutter that I felt paralyzed, not knowing how to act to deal with the mountain of problems. Like I was looking at a ten-thousand-piece puzzle, and even worse, I was sure there were missing pieces. Let me elaborate so you understand.

Emotionally, I was still a wreck. The truth is, I still had more reasons to be depressed than happy with my healing. Although it was healed in my physique, the depression did not miraculously disappear. My wife was still sick and battling bone marrow cancer. This obviously affected me since she is not only my wife but my best friend and companion. To see her sick and in pain without being able to help her affected me a lot emotionally.

In addition, she was the one who managed the finances of our household. Her profession is that of a Certified Accountant, and for her, that part was easy and came naturally. For me it was a very difficult task to do, which is why it took its tow on me emotionally. The pressure was overwhelming, and I was struggling to resume any kind of stability in our lives. Topping it off, because of the depression, I didn't even have the desire to get out of bed.

I was unemployed and without much hope. I was applying

everywhere. Visiting job agencies, posting my resume on various websites, and inquiring about opportunities from former professional colleagues; I was doing it all. None of these efforts panned out. The pressure compounded as the Unemployment Compensation benefits were about to expire. The unemployment check did not even cover our basic bills and living expenses, but it was better than nothing. My credit score, which was once amazing, had dropped to an all-time low. I already had more than $50,000 in overdue medical bills. During the eight years of illness, we lost all our material possessions (our house was foreclosed, all the furniture that was in storage was lost, etc.) All our savings and retirement funds had been exhausted. Income taxes were not filed for three years. Simple things like car registration had not been done for years. Things were usually handled by my wife but were now neglected since we were both sick.

In summary, we were not living. We were just surviving day by day. If I were to go into more detail, I'd have to write another book just on this topic. I think I've said enough for you to understand that our financial life was in ruin.

Spiritually, I was broken. My faith in God never wavered, but in my heart, I had given up a long time ago. I simply accepted that it was God's will for me to remain sick. The voices of trouble and doubt were drowning out God. I was no longer able to hear His voice. Only when I hit rock bottom, at times even contemplating suicide, the subtle voice of the Holy Spirit echoed in my heart:

— "My son. Don't do that. I still have a purpose in your life."

I can't explain how I was sure that it was God, except that it was enough to renew my strength, no matter how small, to go on one more day.

After receiving healing, I began to feel an inexplicable desire to seek Him more, but I didn't know how to begin. Inside, I cried out for Him, yet my lips were frozen. There were no words, and I couldn't pray. But I'm thankful that when it comes to seeking God, nothing depends solely on us. When we are able, we can act, yet there are times when we can do absolutely nothing, and in those moments, God, in His infinite love, does.

"In the same way, the Spirit helps us in our weakness. We do not know what we ought to pray for, but the Spirit himself intercedes for us through wordless groans. And he who searches our hearts knows the mind of the Spirit, because the Spirit intercedes for God's people in accordance with the will of God." Romans 8:26,27 (NIV)

So, I asked Him:

— "What now, Lord?"

And He answered:

— "Wait and see, my son... Wait and see."

8. Seek First...

This chapter will sound ironic at first. That is because it will appear to contradict everything I've said so far. Another paradox is that I've been focusing on the hidden realms of our being. Emotional and spiritual. Then, urging you to respond by acting in the physical world. While still advising you that you cannot reach the emotional or the spiritual directly.

For me, and I believe it will be the same for all, the transformation truly began when I first sought His Kingdom. Recalling again the instructions from our Messiah: **"But seek first his kingdom and his righteousness, and all these things will be given to you as well"** in **Matthew 6:33**. He never said, "seek only," but He said, "seek first." This means we must seek these spiritual things through action but still start with the spiritual. That is the logical progression to reap the promised result. The proper way to heed His instruction.

Let me make this jumbled mess a bit clearer: You should not seek only the Kingdom. That is, don't just pray and read your Bible. You need to act and live in righteousness. However, you still need to seek first the Kingdom. That is, begin with prayer and know His Word and will. According to scripture, there is no other way to live righteously.

Now that I fully comprehended this, I was ready to begin. The funniest thing was how God initiated this "conversation" with me. How He prompted me to begin this walk. Understand this: God speaks as He wills. Scriptures show Him using a mule to speak to a prophet. He will certainly communicate with you and I in a way that we will have no doubt He has spoken. The reason I even bring this up is because, unfortunately, God's own people seem to limit Him the most. I know that many will probably judge what I'm about to testify. However, since that is how it happened, then that is how I'm going to share it. Here we go:

Disney had just released the movie "Frozen 2," and I decided to watch it with my daughter Isabella. I didn't have any expectations about the film or its message. My only intention was to spend an afternoon away from home with my daughter, who was looking forward to seeing the continuation of Elsa and Anna's story. If you haven't seen the movie yet, I'm already warning you that I'm going to spoil the ending here, as I must tell you what happened. But I don't think that will be a problem, because if you have children, you've probably seen the movie a dozen times. If you don't have any, then you likely don't care enough to even see it (*laughter*).

At the end of the film, Anna was alone and stranded in a dark, ominous cave, feeling completely hopeless. Suddenly, she heard her mother's voice through her memories saying,

— "Take a step and do the right thing."

This memory encouraged and strengthened her to get up and move towards her goal. By these actions, Anna became the heroine of the film. She was established as the big protagonist. My heart burned as I watched this unexpected twist! That is when I heard the voice of the Spirit, soft, within me, say,

— "Take a step and do the right thing, my son."

By the end of the movie, that phrase was permanently stuck in my brain. I couldn't tell you any other part of the plot. However, every time I recalled that scene, I heard again in my heart,

— "Take a step, no matter how small. Do the right thing."

Just as it did for Anna, that statement encouraged me to move forward. In my case, the first step was to acknowledge that I needed help and seek it. Admittedly, this is not an easy step, but as hard as it may be, it is usually the first step. If you cannot recognize that you need a change, it will be nearly impossible to take a step towards such a change.

Once I realized I needed help, I called my doctor and asked him to recommend a psychologist. With that single action, I began to feel better. A sense of accomplishment filled me. It was a baby step, but it was a step forward. The next one was to go to the appointment. And so, it was. One step after another. No matter how small. This initiated a chain reaction of steps that eventually led to my victory.

The process wasn't immediate or easy. I was so debilitated and depressed that, in my daily life, my first baby step was to get out of bed and take a shower. Simple activities that everyone does effortlessly or without thinking was a huge battle for me. But every day that I did them, I felt better, stronger, and empowered to take a bigger step. What I learned is that many times, our obstacles are mental and must be overcome with effort. Your body and mind won't want to do it, but if you put in the effort and do it anyway, you'll see that it wasn't that hard after all.

The next big move I needed to take was calling my family. My family members had been praying for my recovery all this time. I felt restricted from calling them often because every time I spoke to them, I felt worse than before. I know it wasn't out of malice or their intention, but every time they asked the same questions about my health, I gave them the same answers because nothing had changed. After a while, I just stopped calling. I became more depressed because I didn't see a solution, and it was making me sad to have to think about it.

Their prompts made me focus on the problem and not the solution.

Now that I received the healing, the barrier was no longer that, but shame, along with guilt and the feeling of ungratefulness. Later, I realized that those feelings were evil. The enemy of our souls does everything to defeat us by projecting lies into our minds. That's what he did to me. But through prayer and the instruction of the Holy Spirit, I finally mustered up the courage to call them. As I dialed the number, I recall feeling like the prodigal son, rehearsing in my mind my plead for forgiveness for neglecting them. To my surprise, I couldn't utter a single rehearsed word because their joy wouldn't even allow me enough time to ask for forgiveness. It was wonderful! Much like the prodigal son, I was received with open arms and celebration.

Healthy relationships are essential to achieve victory and balance. No one achieves success alone, and who better to fight at your side than your family? I don't know your family situation, but I want to challenge you to contemplate how you can restore relationships in your life. I understand that each circumstance is different, and you know what will be best for your life and family in general. I'm just saying that you should pray and seek God's direction and act in obedience to whatever He shows you. I suspect that based on His character, that reconciliation may be His plan.

Don't listen to opposing feelings or voices in your head. That is why we must seek God's Kingdom and His righteousness to find His will first. I know that sounds cryptic. His will isn't easily defined. Therefore, just as I did, take little steps. Do the right thing, one day at a time. He wants you to change your patterns and lifestyle. I may not know much, but of this, I am certain:

"Do not conform to the pattern of this world, but be transformed by the renewing of your mind. Then you will be able to test and approve what God's will is—his good, pleasing and perfect will." Romans 12:2 (NIV)

When we are in this will, we surrender to His plan. And the Lord's plan and desire is this:

"'For it is I who know the plans I have for you,' declares the Lord, 'plans to prosper you and not to harm you, plans to give you hope and a future.'" Jeremiah 29:11 (NIV)

9. Balance

Years ago, I had such a lucid dream that it was seared into my memory. It was a dream about an event at a local church, a community outreach. It wasn't my own church or known place, though. I recall being at this event with many of my friends who don't even go to church. It was odd, but I believe the Lord was trying to show me something through that dream. The people who were organizing the event were very wise. They knew that nothing attracts a group faster than children and free food. The goal was to bring young couples with children to the church, and in my viewpoint, the event was a success. Made evident by how packed the place was.

My favorite part of the dream occurred when I saw an adorable little boy wearing a black tuxedo while serving food to the crowd. It caught my attention because he looked like a little penguin walking with a cute waddle from side to side. He had a captivating smile and asked the groups he approached,

— "Would you like to eat something?"

I felt immense joy when I saw him serving with such delight. I thought to myself,

— "What an exceptional child!"

He approached our group next and repeated the inquiry to me and my friends. I said:

— "Thank you very much, young man. Your parents must be very proud. Are you having fun serving the Lord?"

I could tell from the boy's face that he was confused. So, I asked:

— "Why don't you answer? Are you shy?"

He said, with conviction:

— "I'm not shy. The problem is that I don't have 'Lord' on my tray. We are only serving pizza and cake now. I am sorry."

Everyone in my group started laughing, but I didn't want to hurt the boy's feelings. I bent down to talk to him face to face and said:

— "No problem. I want a pizza, please. You're doing an excellent job. Keep bringing joy to everyone."

He continued to the next group, all smiles. It was the last scene I remembered from the dream before I woke up. My first reaction was to scratch my head and think,

— "What a crazy dream, with no beginning or end."

But then I started thinking more about the dream. Normally, I never remember my dreams, but the dream was so lucid that it felt more like a memory. As I pondered about the little boy, I laughed out loud. I remembered his specific words and thoughts,

— "Why was he confused by my question?"

After meditating more about it, I extracted two valuable lessons from our interaction in the dream.

The first lesson is that words have meaning and need to be well-defined. If they are not defined or taken out of context, the resulting conversation can change completely. I understood that "serving the Lord" meant "doing something in the name of or for the Lord" and that "Lord" in that context was Jesus. The young man thought that "Lord" was some kind of unfamiliar food. Since he was serving food, he misunderstood the phrase "serving the Lord" to mean that I was asking for some food that he didn't have. It reminded me of the time when my family would go out to eat corn on the cob at the street market in Brazil. One weekend, we were on our way, and my father asked:

— "Are we going to eat green corn?" *Green corn is the street name for corn on the cob in Brazil.

— "I don't want green corn," I replied with a sad and disappointed tone.

— "Why don't you want it?" He asked with a frown of confusion on his face. He knew I really liked to eat corn on the cob, so he was truly surprised.

— "I want yellow corn." I responded.

Everyone in the car started laughing, but I was puzzled. That's when they explained to me that the name of the vegetable was green corn and that they weren't talking about its color.

This brings me to the second lesson: each person is at different levels of maturity, and, depending on the degree of maturity, they may understand things in different ways or even not at all. For this reason, I will take a long time to explain what I write and define the words in this book because I do not know the spiritual maturity of each reader.

If you already know these concepts and are already mature in your walk with God, use this book to reinforce your knowledge. That may not be the case for everyone. Therefore, my goal is for you to understand the message being given. I do not wish to sound condescending and act as if I am wiser and more knowledgeable than others. Just as Jesus, through His parables, illustrated the Kingdom of God in practical ways, I will attempt to do the same. This is so you or anyone else may apply the lessons in your lives and reap the benefits of obedience to God.

Allow me to share an illustration with another personal story:

In 1984, a movie came out that changed the lives of countless young men, including me. I was 10 years old at the time, but I remember it as if it was yesterday. Coming out of the movie theater, full of inspiration to overcome the problems I was going through at school. Although this was often not addressed at that time, most students went through a significant common dilemma: bullying.

The movie I'm describing, "The Karate Kid," touched on this very subject. If you've never seen this movie, I encourage you to watch it because it's worth it. I'll try not to spoil your experience too much, but I also think it's been a few decades, and the "spoiler alert" rule no longer applies. It's a movie about a skinny kid named Daniel who had just relocated to a new state and was enrolled in a new school. Daniel was having a tough time adjusting to his new environment. At this school, a group of young men were constantly bullying him. To make matters worse, they all knew karate. The moral of the story was how Daniel overcame the problem with the help of an old man named Miyagi, a karate master from Okinawa. The most wonderful part of the film was that Daniel learned many things during his journey to redemption. He learned how to stand up for himself while honoring his teacher, not through revenge, but by finding balance in his life. The movie got me excited because I, and probably so many teenagers, were able to identify with it. We lived through Daniel's eyes.

Thinking about this movie now and after my dream made me chuckle once again (I think if anyone were observing me, they'd think I was crazy with all these solo laughing sessions). At one point in the film, while teaching about balance through a karate lesson, Miyagi tells Daniel,

— "Daniel-San, whole life has balance... if you walk right side safe... walk left side safe... walk middle... Squish just like grape, understand?" with a heavy accent but stern voice.

Daniel replies with a slightly confused expression,

— "Yes, I think I understand."

It didn't make sense to me at the time. I remember watching this scene when I was 10 years old, and what I was thinking:

— "Shut up, old man, and teach the boy karate already. And learn to speak proper English while you're at it." Annoyed at the lengthy conversations that didn't make sense to me.

It was a sincere reaction from a 10-year-old. Now I understand that what Miyagi was trying to teach Daniel is that all of life needs balance. If you don't walk in the middle of the road and make sure the right and left sides are safe, you'll get crushed like a grape. It is a principle of life. Something I would never understand at the age of 10.

Myth: The Bible has unique information that is difficult to understand and apply.

As noted above, I mentioned that Jesus often used parables while speaking in public. Parables are figurative stories that use familiar things to describe and explain unknown things. Many of his parables begin with the phrase "the kingdom of God is like..." and use something common of the time to describe heavenly things. The parallels helped the nomadic people to understand more complex issues. None of us have ever seen heaven, so Jesus used earthly devices to illustrate heavenly principles.

Sometimes, even after Jesus illustrated something with parables, the audience wouldn't make the connections. Later, He would further clarify the parable to His disciples and followers. I used to think,

— "How is this fair? Why is God giving more information to some than to others? How can He judge justly if not all have the same knowledge?"

But now I understand that God never does that. He explained things to His followers simply because they asked Him. They wanted more and stayed with Him long after everyone else left. These individuals had a deeper, more intimate relationship with Him and a higher level of maturity and commitment. You can have the same relationship too. All it takes is desire.

God gives to those who seek. If you seek to understand the Scriptures, He is always willing to teach you. If you spend more time with Him, you will receive more revelation. It's that simple.

"Consider it pure joy, my brothers and sisters, whenever you face trials of many kinds, because you know that the testing of your faith produces perseverance. Let perseverance finish its work so that you may be mature and complete, not lacking anything. If any of you lacks wisdom, you should ask God, who gives generously to all without finding fault, and it will be given to you." James 1:2-5 (NIV)

Let's go back to defining balance. The word "balance" can have many different meanings and may differ for each person. Since I don't want to have any abstract concepts in this book, I will define it in the context addressed by this book. I am talking about a life that brings balance between body, soul, and spirit. That is a balance between the physical and the spiritual realms. We will need both to solve any problem in life. With the clarity that everything ultimately manifests itself in the physical reality. We need to understand that we only have access to our bodies and the physical world around us. Because our body is the expression of everything we go through. If we need to improve our mental or emotional health, we must still change habits that involve using our bodies. Getting more rest, sleep, and having healthier relationships. All these are done through the body and the world around us. The same goes if we wish to improve our spiritual lives. We must pray, read the Bible, meditate and fast. All things done through the body. So, to access the mind, heart, soul and spirit, you still need the body and action in the earthly realm. You still need to change a physical habit. Everything we think and feel is through our bodies. The body is the instrument we use to interact with the world and with others.

I have made an illustration below to make it easier for you to understand and for you to visualize what I am trying to express:

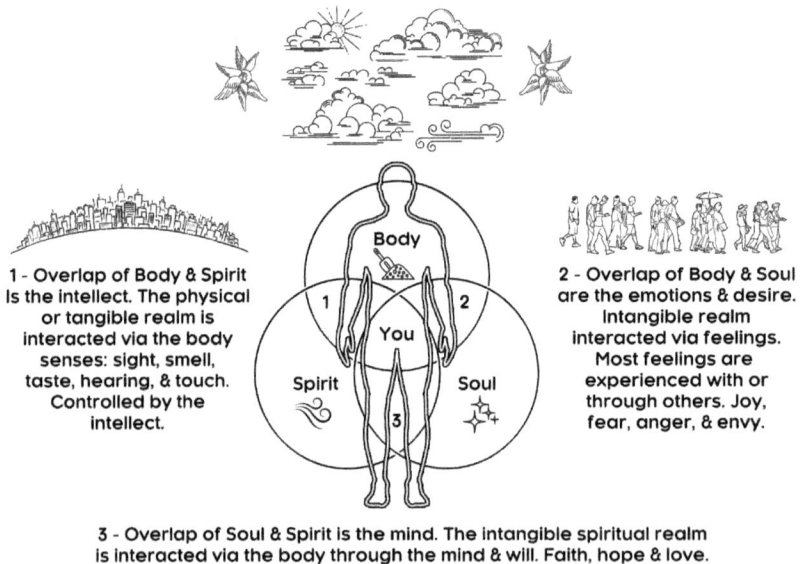

1 - Overlap of Body & Spirit is the intellect. The physical or tangible realm is interacted via the body senses: sight, smell, taste, hearing, & touch. Controlled by the intellect.

2 - Overlap of Body & Soul are the emotions & desire. Intangible realm interacted via feelings. Most feelings are experienced with or through others. Joy, fear, anger, & envy.

3 - Overlap of Soul & Spirit is the mind. The intangible spiritual realm is interacted via the body through the mind & will. Faith, hope & love.

Just as God is complex, so are you, for you were created in His image and likeness. You are more than your physical body, but through it, you access other parts of your life and all aspects of the reality around you, both visible and invisible. The Bible clearly teaches us that there are visible and invisible things and that Adonai, the Creator, is the Master of them all:

"The Son is the image of the invisible God, the firstborn over all creation. For in him all things were created: things in heaven and on earth, visible and invisible, whether thrones or powers or rulers or authorities; all things have been created through him and for him." Colossians 1:15-16 (NIV)

But it also teaches us that everything that is invisible manifests itself in the visible:

"For since the creation of the world God's invisible qualities—his eternal power and divine nature—have been clearly seen, being understood from what has been made, so that people are without excuse." Romans 1:20 (NIV)

And that invisible things are eternal, and so we should keep them in mind during our pilgrimage on earth:

"So, we fix our eyes not on what is seen, but on what is unseen, since what is seen is temporary, but what is unseen is eternal." 2 Corinthians 4:18 (NIV)

The ultimate lesson is that to gain balance, we must remember to maintain all areas of our lives in well-being. While not losing focus that our ultimate vision must be linked to eternal things — the things of the Father.

Here are some examples of people who operate in the extremes of their ego. Remember that these are just illustrations, but if you fit into one of them, don't worry. Almost everyone will shift between these states during their lifetime. If you find yourself in one of these states, begin your journey to balance yourself. These extremes distort our view of the world around us, their consequences are negative, and they almost always bring division between groups of people. They are:

The super emotional: A person who makes serious and often big decisions based on how the immediate result makes them feel without thinking about the future consequences. This person usually ends up addicted to euphoria and immediate gratification, so they move from experience to experience, trying to recapture the feeling of immediate satisfaction. It is a very common state among adolescents, teens, and young adults. It usually manifests as uncontrollable addictions like drugs, video games, sex, and relationships that aren't healthy (among countless other self-destructive things).

At the opposite extreme, we have:

The super-rational: This type of person lives by logic and neglects any aspect of reality that cannot be proven by science or experienced by their five senses. If it cannot be touched, smelled, felt, seen, or heard, they assume that it does not exist or that it must have some explanation that has not yet been discovered. In general, these people have few relationships or relationships based on convenience. They are intellectuals and well-educated, and that is why the world usually treats them with indifference. They also have difficulty relating with others and showing compassion or empathy.

And lastly, we have:

The super-spiritual: This extreme is often the most dangerous. They are the people who live "free" and make decisions based on their faith or religion. If something doesn't align with their point of view, they reject it. This type of person lives in two extremes simultaneously: either they say that God forgives everything and doesn't care about sin, or they say that God is a Judge who condemns every act without grace and love. They live in the extreme of grace or in the extreme of legalism. Both are incorrect.

I call these extremes because, well, they are. I don't think anyone person is in one of these states, but they probably encompass a combination of them. Even if you find yourself engulfed in one of these extremes, recognizing it and taking action to get out is the essential first step. Resolve these issues one small step at a time. In future chapters, I will talk about practical ways to come up with a plan and execute it. For now, it is sufficient to learn about these extremes before seeking balance.

Speaking of balance, there's another iconic scene in the Karate Kid movie, closer to the end, where Miyagi asks Daniel:

— "Do you remember the lesson on balance?"

Daniel nodded.

— "The lesson isn't for karate only. It's a lesson for all life. All life needs balance... Do you understand?"

He shows him a picture of Allie, the girl Daniel had been flirting with. Daniel smiled and said:

— "Yes... I understand."

Daniel had a conflict with Allie that he had not resolved, so his life was out of balance.

I agree with Miyagi. The smallest things throw our lives out of balance. We tend to ignore them, but if we don't deal with them, they will either become giants or accumulate into compounding troubles. We must always act to find a resolution as soon as possible, no matter how small the issue is.

One last thing I'd like to address about balance that is often ignored: the balance between activities and rest. The Creator Himself gave us this lesson from the very beginning in Bereshit (Genesis). He created the world, and on the seventh day, he rested from all the work he had done. He sanctified and consecrated the seventh day as a sign to be observed. Why and for what purpose did God do this? He, being Almighty, did not need to rest. Even the Bible itself reveals this:

"He will not let your foot slip he who watches over you will not slumber; indeed, he who watches over Israel will neither slumber nor sleep." Psalm 121:3-4 (NIV)

Yet God chose to rest as an example to remind us that resting is essential. If we don't replenish the energy spent and allow our tank to go on empty, we won't be able to proceed. In all of the above areas, we need to receive in order to give. We cannot give in the emotional, spiritual or physical spheres if we do not receive it from the Lord. The source of life and everything is Jesus. He is the true Vine. So, we must remain attached to Him, or we will perish.

"I am the vine; you are the branches. If you remain in me and I in you, you will bear much fruit; apart from me you can do nothing." John 15:5 (NIV)

We need to rest in all areas, but resting the body is essential. Good habits such as going to bed early, sleeping well, resting the mind, and even doing nothing are essential to achieve victory in work and daily life. Take moments to go for a walk and appreciate nature and the Father's creation. We live in a time and culture that demands we always stay busy. Most people wake up and immediately get on social media. Many even take showers with their cell phones because of the fear of missing out (FOMO). Always busy, running around, but getting nowhere. Resetting our bodies is not optional.

Many also neglect our emotional state. Replenish your soul by investing in relationships. Stop and play with your children. Have a picnic with your spouse. Call your mom or best friend and talk to him or her for an hour. These emotional connections and intimate relationships restore our emotional tank.

Lastly, and potentially the most important, rest your spirit in the presence of the Most High. Even Jesus disappeared frequently to spend time alone with the Father. He is the Source of life. That is the meaning of "resting" in the Lord.

"Whoever dwells in the shelter of the Most High will rest in the shadow of the Almighty. I will say of the Lord, 'He is my refuge and my fortress, my God, in whom I trust.'" Psalms 91:1,2 (NIV)

10. Organization

Once I began to seek first the Kingdom of God, many of my situations began to change, and opportunities manifested themselves. It was the beginning of my journey towards achieving balance, and it can be yours as well. I persisted in prayer, seeking the Lord's direction and acting when the answers presented themselves. It was then that I detected a pattern: The opportunities were serving as the Spirit's confirmation that guided me through the process.

Of course, I had my own priorities in mind. As most people tend to rationalize, the highest priority would be to find a job and have a steady flow of income. The mindset of the world has always been that money solves everything. I quickly discovered that God had other plans. He knew that first, my physical health, my emotional state, and even my mental health had to be restored. My spirit was being strengthened, but the rest of my being still suffered the side effects from 8 years of constant struggle.

Today, I understand that if He had allowed me to find a job right away, I would have failed. I was in no condition to do anything consistently yet. What God allowed me to do was a self-diagnosis and internal examination. I was undergoing my psychological treatment while also decreasing the doses of the medications that had been in my system for so long. I suddenly realized that I had to start everything from scratch. The extent of my vulnerability was so vast that I even had to re-learn how to eat. Psychologically, my body and mind were in defense mode. I spent so much time in terrible pain after eating that even ingesting small amounts was very difficult, both physically and mentally. He had a plan for me, and it was a lot slower than I had expected.

As part of my early recovery, I began taking daily walks around my neighborhood. To maximize my efforts, I would also listen to worship hymns while praising the Creator on these strolls. Some days, I would also spend the time talking to my friends and family. These actions helped me re-establish many of my broken relationships, which aided in healing my emotional state.

My daughter, Isabella, was a big part of my recovery. Even during my illness, I did everything I could to keep my promise to God to be a good father. But now, restored, I focused even more on my relationship with her. In the morning, I got into the habit of waking up earlier to get her ready for school. During the week, I became more committed to her activities by driving her to dance, art and gym classes. Also ensuring she went to church services and events during the week. We would spend hours playing and talking once she got home from school. All the happiest moments of my life have involved her. To my surprise, I learned something very profound during this period: God can often use children to teach us. Never think that your children have nothing to offer you; God uses whomever He wants. Children are innocent and obedient, which is why they are actually God's perfect candidates.

My life became a personal university. I began to learn from everything around me, including about divine providence. I spent more than a year unemployed, and our family lacked nothing. We didn't have to rely on people's good will either. Somehow, and to be honest, I still don't fully understand it. He provided for all our needs. The time God gave me to recover was the foundation upon which I built the life we live today. Without this foundation, I wouldn't have ever attained fulfillment. It gave me an undeniable faith that He is true to His word and that I can trust Him.

All I have expressed so far has been personal. A testimony

of what God has done in my life and will not necessarily apply to most people's situations. What I'm going to share from now on is a system that can be applied in any circumstance of life. This includes your life if you so desire. It isn't something I invented but something I have learned and applied. I can tell you without a doubt that this system works. Here is the moment you've been waiting for, so take out your notepad. It's not rocket science, either. Most of these things are common sense knowledge. That is good news because anyone can do it.

The first principle is organization.

I had so many tasks to accomplish that I didn't know where to begin.

— "What do I do and how?" I asked myself.

I knew I would have to come up with a plan before I could act. I know this as a biblical principle that is very practical. Here's what Jesus says about it:

"Suppose one of you wants to build a tower. Won't you first sit down and estimate the cost to see if you have enough money to complete it? For if you lay the foundation and are not able to finish it, everyone who sees it will ridicule you, saying, 'This person began to build and wasn't able to finish.'" Luke 14:28-30

My career is in Project Management through Technology and Software. For that reason, I learned to apply a lot of tools and techniques from my profession to my personal life. God afforded me the wisdom to employ my experience in this area of my life into any goal. After all, everything in our lives is a project. The definition of a project, even within the profession, is: "a temporary endeavor undertaken to create a unique service or outcome." It is necessary to have a goal that can be achieved after a specific period with a palpable result. For example, if your goal weight is 120lbs, and you currently weigh 140lbs, then you can say that you are on a personal project to lose 20lbs. It is that simple. As long as your goal is clear and not ongoing, you can treat it as a project.

Once you have set a goal, you must break the goal down into smaller steps. In Project Management, we call these "SMART" goals. The letters in the word SMART form an instructive acronym. Each letter of the word S.M.A.R.T. has specific instructions to qualify the goal as "smart." Here they are:

S – Small: The goal should be something small and specific.

M – Measurable: The goal should be something that can be measured and have a clear outcome.

A – Attainable: The goal should be something that can be achieved.

R – Relevant: The goal should be something that makes a difference in your life.

T – Time-Based: The goal should be something you can achieve in a specific time and reasonably short period.

Anyone can apply this concept to any personal goal. Just break down any goal into smaller steps until it becomes a smart goal: small, measurable, attainable, relevant, and achievable in a reasonable amount of time. Initially, my goals were so small that they had to be achieved on the same day. Getting up, bathing, eating, praying, reading the Bible, walking, and talking to people who have added to my life. Over time, these tasks became easier to accomplish as they became habits, and I started thinking about bigger, more complex goals. No matter where you are today, there are always objectives you can achieve. The hardest part is getting started. The good news is that, like me, anyone can start now with things you manage. These small steps will change how you think and perceive victory. Before you realize it, you will become conditioned to win and desire more. Like the dogs in the Pavlov experiment, we spoke about earlier. Growing little by little.

Myth: Downtime is wasted time.

The time I spent standing still, analyzing my life and recovering, for many, may seem like wasted time. On the contrary, I learned that this was another lie from the enemy and a necessary hiatus.

I'm not saying that the same is going to happen to everyone, but if you find yourself in a similar situation where God is directing you to wait on Him, don't ever think of that period as wasted time. For me, it was a time when God used to bring me many personal revelations and give me new dreams. I learned to depend on Him more than ever before.

I began to write down everything that was going through my mind and organize the turmoil of my life. These problems and dreams became my bucket list. Next, I put a label indicating which one I should pursue. The labels were "golden nuggets," "foolish pursuits," or "unicorns" (*laughter*). Let me explain:

These labels were adopted from my phase of watching Christian apologetics debates with militant atheists. One of the many videos I watched made me laugh hysterically as the atheist posed the following question:

— "How can you believe such an old-fashioned book that even talks about unicorns as if they were real?"

Of course, the passages (there are nine: **Numbers 23:22** and **24:8, Deuteronomy 33:17, Job 39:9-10, Psalms 22:21,29:6,** and **92:10,** and **Isaiah 34:7**) that talk about the unicorn were probably referring to a wild rhinoceros or buffalo. To this day, in science, the one-horned rhinoceros has the scientific name unicorn for this breed. But the atheist was thinking of the mystical animal, a white horse with a horn on its forehead, which has magical abilities and is considered beautiful and perfect. And because of that, I began to label any target or goal that cannot be achieved as a unicorn. Unicorns are not smart goals, as they cannot be achieved except through a miracle. They are mythical.

Fact: Eliminate every unicorn from your life. It will only bring you frustration and keep you away from the golden nuggets.

Here's my list as an example, originally written in 2017:

1. Pay off all my debt – gold nugget.
2. Purchase a new car – foolish pursuit.
3. Learn a new language (at the time, it was Greek) – golden nugget.
4. Travel around the world – unicorn.
5. Learn to play the piano – golden nugget.
6. Play video games as a profession (streaming) – foolish pursuit.
7. Generate a financial income on YouTube – foolish pursuit.
8. Write a book – golden nugget.
9. Read more books – golden nugget.
10. To be used by God through miracles (cures, etc.) foolish pursuit.

I will now elaborate on the logic behind my labels. Remember, these were the top ten goals on my original list. After reflecting on each item and understanding why they came to mind, I applied the appropriate labels. The main reason I created a list was to help me organize my thoughts and focus on the important items. The list and analytical process aided me in seeing which of them was worth the effort. My goals are going to have different values than yours. It is supposed to be personal. However, for the strategy to work, you must be honest with yourself. For clarity's sake and to serve as a practical example to you, let me justify my own decisions:

Item 2, "buying a new car," was labeled as a foolish pursuit for the following reason: I already had a car, and it was in good condition. I wanted a new one, but I didn't need one. We all need transportation, and because of that, a car can be a necessity. In my case, it was a desire instead of a need.

Item 4, "travel around the world," was marked as a unicorn. Not because traveling and getting to know other cultures is not something good that I desired, but my goal was not specific enough and, therefore, impossible to achieve. Even without money limitations, I couldn't travel all over the world. A new option, which I even substituted on my list, was: "travel to Israel with my family." Don't forget that your goals must be smart goals. Otherwise, they become unicorns.

Items 6 and 7 were goals that could be achieved, but they required a lot of time and dedication. Furthermore, they didn't focus on what was important to my life. They were things I liked to do, but the more I thought about them, the more I realized that the reasons were selfish. They didn't align with my decision to glorify God in my pursuits. That is why I have called them foolish pursuits.

The last one, and probably the one that must have confused many people, is item 10, "being used by God for miracles, such as healing." As you have seen, I labeled this as a foolish pursuit. Why? As a Christian, shouldn't this be the main goal of all believers? This is exactly why I pointed out that we must be honest with ourselves for this system to work. Did I put this on the list for the glory of God or for personal reasons? We all want to be used by God, but almost no one wants to pay the price to reach that status. So, I revised the goal to "know and learn to serve God with all my heart, mind, and strength to be used by God according to His will," to "improve my relationship with God." If it is with a gift of healing, let it be a gift of healing. If it's cleaning the church bathroom, let it be cleaning the church bathroom. The important thing is not what I want but what He wants for me.

Fact: Don't despise small beginnings. God's plans are not always easy to see. Trust Him.

This was a long chapter because it addressed an important topic. I want to tie it all together with the focus of the book: achieving wholeness. This and the next few lessons will be very practical. Activities that you can apply in the same way to your life if you choose. Organizing and planning is a crucial step in managing and achieving goals. You can apply these steps verbatim or modify them in a way that makes more sense to you or aligns with your personal goals. The important thing is to always remember to focus on balance. The lessons are physical, but don't neglect the spiritual side. Always balance your actions with prayer. Allow time to receive guidance and instructions from the Holy Spirit. Make an initial list of everything that comes to your mind, no matter how absurd it may seem. Dreaming is part of the process. Then pray and seek God's direction, and He will help you adjust your list, laying out a plan to achieve the results.

It's wonderful to have God as a partner. And to know that, with Him, everything we do is guaranteed to excel. There will be struggles but also many victories. Rest assured.

11. Priorities

Now that you have a defined list of goals and you've pulled out the ones that don't suit you, the next step is to put them in order of priority. It would be wonderful if it were possible to do everything on our lists right away, but that's not realistic. The reality is that you can only put your focus on one or two items at a time, making it imperative that you start with the most important items. Continue to review your list wisely, always seeking God first and listening to the guidance of the Holy Spirit and trusted peers.

It isn't something that is immediately obvious. For instance, and as I have previously stated, in my human understanding I felt the priority was money. So, I set out to look for work. It is in our nature to always prioritize physical needs over anything else. When these are not being met, it is absolutely normal to become obsessed with the issue at hand. We can become consumed by it if we are not careful. Dedicating all our time and effort to that one thing, and when we are not doing something, we tend to think about it. The worry can hinder us even from sleeping and from accomplishing other things.

As I acted and continued to pray, I quickly realized that this was not His immediate plan for my situation. I felt Him saying in my heart, "Not yet, and don't worry, for I will provide." How could I be sure that this voice was really from the Spirit? Based on two principles: The first is that I was doing everything within my power. I was applying and looking for work in every way possible and in everything, seeking the Lord in prayer. Remembering that He will never do things that we are able to do for ourselves, we can rest knowing that when we do our part, He will take care of us. If you do your part and do not achieve the hoped result while remaining in His path, you can be at peace, which is in fact, the second principle. The inexplicable peace that surpasses all understanding described in the scriptures. Jesus said this regarding our physical needs:

"Look at the birds of the air; they do not sow or reap or store away in barns, and yet your heavenly Father feeds them. Are you not much more valuable than they? Can any one of you by worrying add a single hour to your life?" Matthew 5:26-27 (NIV)

Because of this I was not afraid or worried and was convinced that the voice I had heard within me was that of the Holy Spirit. These are things you learn to identify over time as you walk with Him.

I can only describe this mode of communication as a pattern. A pattern that you begin recognizing as you experience Him over the years. When you observe this pattern, your best option is to surrender to the Father's will. Keep doing what is in your power, but trust in Him and His provision. And so, I did. Still, I kept applying for positions every morning for about an hour before shifting my focus to the next task on my list. I continued waiting and trusting the Lord regarding provision and my need to find employment. Instead of being afraid or doubtful, I spent my time praising and glorifying God for His providence.

I need to add an important note here. My testimony should not be used to avoid responsibility or accountability. This is how it happened in my life in this unusual circumstance, and it was confirmed by what happened during the events I'm describing here. I trusted His provision and guidance during those moments, and I can testify that He did not disappoint me. Today, for instance, I'm in a completely different phase and wouldn't just quit my job without absolute confirmation from His part. I wouldn't simply do what I feel or want to test His provision.

My next immediate target was to organize and clean the home. I still didn't have a clear direction on what I would prioritize from my list, so I began laying the ground work until I did. I chose this target for two separate reasons. The environment you are in has a huge impact on your mental wellbeing. It would be difficult to begin focusing on my list without first setting up my surroundings for success. The other reason was to begin doing things that had immediate impact and success. This is especially helpful if you are dealing with something that is out of your control. Something that is important or troubling you and you've done all you can. In my case, it was job seeking. I learned that if you move your attention to something you can do and see immediate results, it will boost your drive and self-esteem. Try to find anything that is productive and achievable. As a bonus, fill your mind with positive thoughts while doing it. I find it extremely helpful to pop in your favorite worship tunes and praise God while doing mundane tasks. I guarantee that you will feel better and you will produce something good, no matter how small.

Fact: God cares about cleanliness and organization.

Most, even if they don't admit or realize this, will find it is hard to feel motivated and inspired to do anything in the middle of the mess. I understand that everyone is different and has their own methods, but this fact is universal. Even people who can work in a clutter quickly learn that they are more productive when they get organized. One may think that taking the time to plan, organize, and clean is wasted. The truth is that the time taken to plan ends up saving us time in the long run.

An added benefit to accomplishing these smaller goals is that it gives us immediate results and pleasure. Every time we get these results, our bodies release pleasure chemicals into our system. We may even end up getting addicted to doing good. The same dopamine lesson I talked about in a previous chapter, specifically when speaking about social media, also applies to any situation that brings us satisfaction. These small victories have the same effects on your brain and create a connection between the good habits and their feelings of accomplishment. That is why I insist that small actions have a large impact over time.

A long time ago, during a business seminar, I learned an interesting lesson. The difference between the elite in any profession or competitive sport from their average counterpart is only about 2%. How so? Most people around the world do what is necessary and give 98% of themselves, but those who go the extra mile and give 100% are the ones who become Olympic athletes or professional football players. They become the best at their chosen craft or the famous singers and movie stars. Just imagine, if we make that little extra effort every day, we can be the best in whatever area we choose to dedicate ourselves to. The reality is that most don't put in the effort to do that. Many give up prematurely or along the way. This lesson is valuable enough that I chose to impress it into my daughter's mind. I always tell her that anything worth doing is worth doing well. I also model this to her in my daily life. Even if I never get famous or rich, this is the life I choose to live. A dedicated life. The very fruit in our lives is sufficient to make it worthwhile. Most important and significant is that He, our Father, sees it.

I'll give you a practical example:

A husband who works hard, provides for his family, cooperates at home, educates his children, is faithful to his wife, and helps his spouse achieve her dreams would be considered a tremendous husband by his family and those around him. But if this husband also pays attention to the small details, such as speaking words of love to his wife every day, bringing flowers from time to time, playing with his children, and calling his wife during the day to say hello, he will be the husband of the year. These smaller daily acts, which are deemed to be insignificant for most, are the things that will draw people's attention in the end. These small deeds are the steps that set him apart from the others who are just performing their obligation. No one can deny that the first husband is excellent and is doing his duty well, but I assure you that if most women had the choice between the two, they would likely choose the latter. That 2% difference is huge over the course of a lifetime. Identify what the 2% is in your life and goals, and make a habit out of purposefully pursing them. Failing to do these minimal things just adds up to missed opportunities and missed potential outcomes.

The practical lesson for this chapter is for you to notice the little things you can do in the moments when you are worried about the ones you can't. Not only will this prevent you from getting stressed, but it will also help you change your daily habits. Remember the experiment about Pavlov's dogs? Your brain will get used to these habits, and the effect is that your body releases hormones that control your emotions. When you find something good that brings you joy, it becomes a habit worth exercising. Wash the dishes after using them. Put things in their proper place. Take out the trash. Clean. Organize. These are a few examples of small activities that bring immediate satisfaction when accomplished. And, husbands, these little things will make your spouse very happy, and if they are happy, you'll be happier, too. This tip is on the house (pun intended *laughter*).

I believe that lays down the groundwork, allowing us to go back to the main topic of this chapter: setting priorities. Often, the process begins with an inquiry. This is the question I asked myself:

— "What is a good functional way to weigh the value and order of the items we should prioritize from our list?"

I personally find it helpful to visualize my goals. So, I used a process from my profession called the Stakeholder Matrix. In the area of Project Management, this matrix is used to understand how we should manage the people affected by the project. I've modified the matrix process so it can be used to gauge my personal goals in a visual style. The original matrix looks like this:

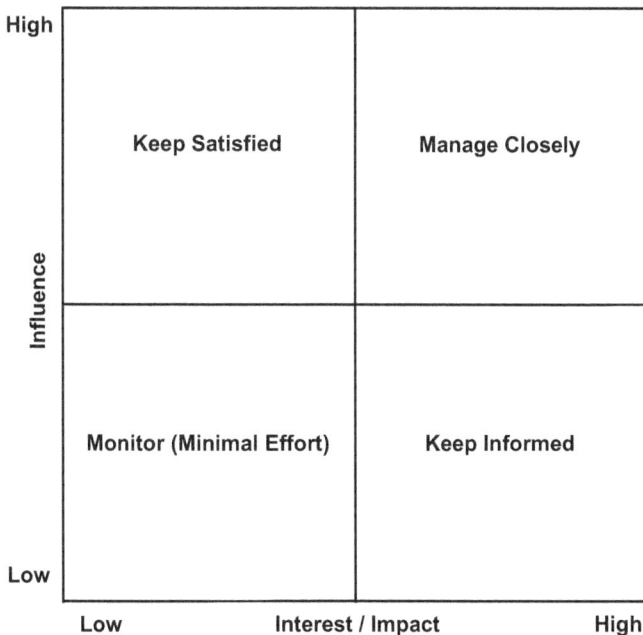

I modified the axis and their respective results on the graph to help me indicate what is important for my life. Next,

I placed my personal goals within this version of the matrix. Here is how it looked after my modifications (keep in mind that this was my initial list of goals from 2017):

	Low Important / Benefit	High Important / Benefit
High Urgency / Time Sensitive	**Do as soon as possible** Car registration	**Tackle immediately** Relationship God Car insurance Find a job
Low Urgency / Time Sensitive	**Do when possible** Write book Read books Piano Greek	**Important, but can wait** Income Taxes Pay off debts

Take note that I added some new items that weren't on my original list from the previous chapter. Putting them down on paper helped me decide what I could or should do first. But remember that this list is based on what's important to my life and only applied to me at that moment. Your priorities may be totally different, and needs evolve over time. An example from my list that may be different from yours is the item of paying off debts. For me, I placed this item very high in importance and benefits but very low in urgency because it is something that must be done but can wait. I also considered what I can and cannot do. At the time I made the list and the priority matrix, I didn't even have a job. So, even if I put the item up there at the highest priority and urgency, I wouldn't be able to do it at that moment. Making it a goal that cannot be achieved and that would have kept me from the achievable ones. For that reason, I set other smaller goals as the immediate priority. Goals such as getting car insurance and finding a job.

Now, with everything prioritized and planned, my life no longer felt as chaotic. The time I spent planning helped me execute everything effectively and smoothly. Often, we become paralyzed and overwhelmed with the complexity and number of troubles we face. The time set aside to plan and organize is time well invested. No matter where your life is right now, visualize a future and write down goals and steps to accomplish them. Prioritize and organize these steps and move forward. One goal at a time. Do this, and I can almost guarantee that you will reach your ultimate ambition.

12. Action Items

A hero's journey is not always easy to follow without relating with the hero from beginning to end. If you've watched the movie "Avengers: Endgame" and witnessed Tony Stark, aka Iron Man, give his life to save the universe from the villain Thanos, you will certainly feel the emotion that the scene sought to inspire. But for the faithful followers of the M.C.U., that same scene was likely to provoke the viewer to shed some tears. Why is that? Why did some feel more emotionally connected to the impact of Tony's personal sacrifice?

Casual viewers may have agreed that it was a heroic act, but it was not accompanied by the same strong emotions. The reason is simple: the faithful followers engaged in a decade-long journey portrayed throughout the films. A journey that portrayed Tony as a rich, spoiled, selfish, arrogant, womaniz-ing, self-centered man in the first movie. Then showed his slow transformation into a man who became a responsible husband and father. A man who cared about others and was willing to put his own dreams aside for the benefit of the people he loved. A man who, in the course of the films, failed several times, but after each fall, got up, learned his lesson and improved. A man who changed his way of thinking about the world, about others, and even about himself several times due to circumstances he faced and their subsequent consequences. And in the end, after nine movies, he gave his own life for humanity.

In my opinion, even though it's based on fiction, his act deserved a few tears. We can relate to this character because, deep down, we want to be that kind of person. The story portrayed him as a flawed character with a tremendous redemption arc. It gives us hope because deep down, we all know we are flawed, and we all hope to prove ourselves worthy. It's exciting and inspiring. Everyone who watched the last film could see this, but only those who followed his story from the beginning felt the full impact of his sacrifice.

I'm not saying all this to imply that I'm the hero of my story. Nor that I'm some source of inspiration. The point I'm trying to get across is that I'm going to share with you, in this chapter, only parts of my story in as much detail as possible. It would be impossible to share my entire life's journey with you, but my hope is that the parts I do share inspire you to make a change. Allow it to impact you in a positive way. I also hope that this becomes abundantly clear to you: the hero of my story is not me; it is Christ.

Everything I write here, including the victories, will be for the glory of the Father and to help you be the hero of your story through Him. My goal is to share the victories I achieved through Christ. But with a clear emphasis that these will not come without difficulties and personal effort. What I will share in the following pages is the result of time, dedication, and struggles.

Therefore, it is very important to note that before I achieved victory in many of these areas, I failed several times. I thought about giving up and made a lot of mistakes. Just like Tony in his journey, it was necessary for me to learn to change my mind and reexamine my priorities. To change my way of seeing the world, people, God, and even myself.

Don't be fooled; you'll also fail and think about giving up. But I urge you to not stop. Keep moving forward with your eyes fixed on Jesus, and He will give you the desired outcome.

Without further ado, I will tell you about the beginning of my journey after receiving the divine healing. And what better way to begin than sharing how I developed my most important goal: Improving my relationship with God.

At first, it seems like an easy goal to achieve, but as it stands, this goal is too abstract. To achieve this or any other goal, it is first necessary to make them more concrete and realistic. We must break them down into smaller, practical steps until they become "smart" goals. Before we do that, we must first make our goals align with our life's aspirations. Do this by following these steps:

Make the goal personal: Define the goal in your own words by answering the following questions: What do you want to achieve? If you had to explain the outcome to someone else, how would you do it? How does the goal affect you personally? Why do you want to achieve it? How will it change your life if achieved? Turn a generic goal into a personal goal.

Establish the starting point: Where do you stand in relation to the goal? We can never reach a destination without knowing where we are starting from. Even if you have a map in your hands, you can't get anywhere without knowing your current location in relation to the map. The same applies with respect to your goal. Know your starting point if you want to reach the desired destination.

Establish your point of arrival: Clearly define what you want to achieve. How do you know if you've achieved your goal? What benefit do you plan to get? Remember that smart goals have to be measurable. This means that the result must be tangible.

Once the goal becomes personal and realistic, you can break it down into smart goals. Remember, SMART goals must be small, measurable, attainable, relevant, and time bound. Here is how I transformed my abstract goal into a tangible and personal one:

Initial Generic Goal: To improve my relationship with God.

Make the goal more personal: I want to seek God more intimately in my daily life, to become more sensitive to the voice of the Holy Spirit and to do the will of the Father. I desire to understand the Father's teachings so that I can practice them without deviating from His Word.

Establish Your Starting Point: Currently, I'm a long way from the goal. I am not completely off the path, but because of the circumstances of my illness, I am debilitated in all areas of my life and, therefore, burdened with feelings of failure, fear, and guilt. I'll have to restart from the basics, but I know God will help me.

Establish your Destination or Desired Outcome: My desire is to obtain wholeness in my life through Christ. I know that this can only be achieved with a real lifelong relationship with Christ. In this case, the goal will never be 100% achieved, but I will consider it a success when I establish daily habits that will maintain my relationship with God as the most important one in my life.

Next, I broke down my end goal into even smaller, practical steps:

1. Pray more often.
2. Read and meditate on the Word daily.
3. Praise and worship the Lord daily.
4. Participate in worship services and bible studies more often.

Now, with the goals broken down as SMART goals, we will need to make them into practical steps. To do this, we need to keep splitting the goals even further until each line becomes a task or an action item. An Action Item is another term defined by my profession. It's simply a final to-do list of tasks that can be completed with a single action.

1. Pray more often (daily):
   a. Schedule time on the calendar to pray.
   b. Create a methodology for praying using Jesus' prayer as a model (first thanking and praising the Father, then for other people, and lastly, my needs).
   c. Create a journal or log of prayer requests to track the requests and record the outcomes as He responds.
2. Read the Word daily:
   a. Schedule a specific time on the calendar each morning to study the Bible without interruption.
   b. Schedule a specific time on the calendar to study other sources that enrich the reading of the Word.
   c. Schedule additional time to meditate on all that I studied, giving the opportunity for the Holy Spirit to minister and communicate God's desire back to my heart.
3. Praise the Lord daily:
   a. Wake up every day with worship music and praises to the Lord.
   b. At every opportunity I get, I hear praise music and worship God throughout the day as well.
4. Participate in worship services and bible studies more often:
   a. Try to attend the services that were already scheduled within my church and community homes.

My list is still generic here, but it's meant to be an example of what I did early during my journey. Today, six years after the original list, I've refined it dozens of times. Most of them have become habits. The reason we should put all this effort at the beginning is because it will help us start, and we must start somewhere.

I must add this important sidenote: Don't turn anything into legalism. Be flexible enough to adapt to your everyday situations but also disciplined enough to do your daily steps "religiously." Keep a balanced lifestyle and use your list as a guideline. My goals were just elements that would help me have a better relationship with the Father. They are only steps to achieve the goal. The goal itself is the "relationship" and not the steps. Please always remember that as you pursue any goal.

Another point to keep in mind: quality is more important than quantity. Especially in relationship-oriented goals. Jesus Himself instructed us in this way:

"And when you pray, don't keep repeating the same thing, as the heathen do. They think that no matter how much they speak, they will be heard." Matthew 6:7 (NIV)

Set realistic goals. The list is a means to an end. The "end game" is to create lifelong habits. Especially goals that are intended to be ongoing, like the example above.

More practical and well-defined goals, such as buying a house, finding a job, or getting a certificate, can be accelerated with more extreme steps to be applied for a set time. But the ones you aimed towards a lifelong commitment should be turned into habits that eventually cause the list to fade while the habits remain.

A good example of this concept can be illustrated by the

contrast of two similar goals with totally different desired outcomes.

Goal A: Lose 10lbs.
Goal B: Improve your diet.

Both goals will probably involve modifying your diet. In the first example, you can go on a more extreme diet and eat foods that will help you lose weight quickly. Use a short-term diet that will lower your calorie intake significantly. For the second example, that same approach won't work, as it's impossible to keep it going for a lifetime. Thus, for that goal, it is more beneficial to change one habit at a time until your diet becomes something you can stick to every day. I'll go into more detail about this example in a later chapter.

Lastly, I want to touch on something that is surely going to happen to you. Life and its inconveniences. You're going to create routines and start seeing results, and once everything starts to fall into place, some odd circumstances will arise. You may get sick, lose your job, get discouraged, or face some unforeseen event. If you are mentally prepared, you will know how to deal with these situations. My recommendation, and this is what has worked in my life, is this: don't ever give up. Adapt and start again if you have to. Even a small step forward is better than standing still. In time, everything will pass, and your life will stabilize again.

When something odd happens in my life, and I share it with my best friend, he always responds with:

— "The only thing constant in life is change. This too shall pass."

I'm not sure where he adopted this fortune cookie wisdom from, but it is definitely true. I will talk about some of these in future chapters and how I equipped myself to deal with them. With the same mentality, anyone can do it.

13. Replacing Habits

In our lives, we think that we can overcome a bad habit by force. What ends up happening is that we either give up or end up replacing it with another bad habit. Our daily lives are made up of habits. Thus, we need to identify and eliminate the bad ones. This is never better illustrated than our eating habits. I always laugh when I hear someone say,

— "This year, I'm going to lose weight. I'm going to start a revolutionary diet that's going to give results. I know a lot of people who are following this diet, and it really works."

I don't laugh because I'm cynical or to ridicule the person. I laugh because the statement itself is ignorant. It's ignorant because, whether we know it or not, we're all already on a diet.

Myth: Fad diets work.

The word "diet" means "one's eating habits." Therefore, if you eat and drink anything, then you're on a diet. You may be on a horrible diet, but it's still a diet, nonetheless. In fact, the sad truth is that most people are on a bad diet. Fad diets don't work because they're meant to be temporary. In fact, when we examine them closely, we see that they harm our health in the long run, as they likely neglect part of our body's basic needs. They almost always give good results in the short term, which makes them "famous" and tempting. However, in the long term, you will likely regain all the weight you lost. At times causing you to gain even more weight than before. This has been scientifically proven and easily confirmed by reality. One of the many reasons for this is our metabolism, the mechanism used by the human body to transform food and calories into energy. Please allow me to elaborate.

Our body doesn't have the same concerns as our mind does. Our mind's goals are often linked to the desired outcomes. We wish to be more attractive, to fit back into those jeans, or even to have the noble goal of being healthier. But regardless of the reason contained in our mind, the body only cares about surviving. And because of this, when we radically decrease the amount of food we consume over a period of weeks, it reacts in the form of self-defense.

To survive during a time of scarcity, the body decreases the intensity of burning calories to preserve energy and begins to store more calories in the form of fat. In this sense, when we finish our temporary "diet" of a few weeks or months and start eating normally again, the body's metabolism is super low and converts everything into fat. This causes us to become disappointed and sad, but it usually results in a repeated cycle of trying another new fad diet. It's a terrible cycle and a reality for many people who struggle with their weight. The end result is often the opposite of our desire. Little by little, over a long period of time, we become obese and debilitated. Physically and emotionally.

Fact: You are always on a diet.

What we should try to understand and put into practice is that we are already on a diet; we just need to improve it. Changing our diet is not something we're going to do for a few days or weeks. It must be something we're going to do for a lifetime. That requires us to swap bad habits with good ones. The only way to do this sustainably is to enjoy your diet. You'll never be able to live with these eating habits if there's something about them that you hate. It's a matter of adaptation and flexibility. That is, learning about the workings of one's own body and taste. Then, creating habits that are beneficial and enjoyable. The first principal worth exploring in this particular topic is your motivation. Just wanting to lose weight or improve one's appearance is not enough motivation. Here are some better motivations that can help you with this important lifelong goal:

1. Live a healthy life.
2. Increase your energy level.
3. Increase your self-esteem.
4. Improve your quality of life.

The good news is that when we change our diet with these needs in mind, the byproducts are exactly what many of us desire:

1. You will lose weight.
2. You will feel better.
3. You will look more attractive.

Achieving this goal in this manner will take longer and require discipline and sacrifice. It won't be easy. Still, it's better than the alternative, which is not to change or get stuck in the cycle of diets that don't work. The diets may be successful in the short term, but you will likely have permanent consequences in the long term. Harmful effects that can generate in your mind a feeling of defeat, which will likely affect other areas of your life. Not to mention the horrific health side effects they may generate over time.

Let's keep in mind that this book is not about dieting. I keep emphasizing this for a reason. The book is about living a balanced life and receiving fullness in Christ. These practical illustrations are being shared to help you achieve that balance. From my experience, I've learned that we have an important and active role to play in getting that fullness. That is why I want to give you real-life examples of what worked for me. I'm also presenting a methodology and principles that anyone can apply or modify to fit their own needs and goals.

In the previous chapters, I gave a basic example of how I started my journey. Now, I want to provide more concrete and detailed examples. A healthier diet is something that many need and can relate to. It is a goal that anyone can apply to their lives now and benefit from it. Your health is also a paramount pillar in your life, and success without it is nearly impossible.

Before I proceed, I want you to understand another one of these universal concepts that will need to be understood for you to succeed. This concept is that life has endless potential for complications and that our resources are limited. In the world of Project Management, this is something recognized and is called Project Risks and Project Constraints. We live in a world full of risks and constraints. No project can have unlimited resources.

To carry out a project, we need to consider, at a minimum, the following constraints: time, money, and resources (can be human resources or materials). In my opinion, the biggest one is time because it affects everyone. Someone may have a lot of money and, with it, be able to get more raw materials or human resources to invest more energy into the project. Time, however, is something everyone gets in equal measure. It doesn't matter if you are poor, rich, white, black, young or old; The only time we are guaranteed is the present. We all only get 24 hours a day, and we don't know when our time will run out. That's why I believe that time is the most precious resource. You can exchange time for money and money for resources, but you can never buy back time.

Myth: Time is money.

Time is not money. Time is far more precious than money. If you lose money or material possessions, you may be able to gain them back. In contrast, lost time is lost forever. With that said, you must consider your own personal constraints when setting up your goals. In my case, at the beginning of my journey, I had a lot of time on my hands and very little money or income. So, my plans were based on things I could do with the money I had available. I stretched every penny to its maximum efficiency. Due to these unusual circumstances, I did learn to use my resources more wisely. Most people are unaware of how much they waste on their monthly income until they need to manage it. I'll give examples of this lesson in the chapter where I deal with finances. For now, let's get back to the subject of diet with this new understanding about limited resources.

As I began to change my diet, I quickly realized two things: first, that diet without exercise is not very effective; Second, that when we combine two similar goals, we can save time and resources, often receiving compounding benefits. Since I'm working on modifying my eating habits with the goal of being healthier, including an exercise routine made sense. This would be a perfect example for showing the benefits of combining similar goals. It is something you should keep in mind when creating your goals. When we combine two or more goals, we save, mitigate, and minimize some of our constraints. In this case, we are saving time by doing similar goals and compounding our benefits by getting better results. For this reason, I changed the goal from "improving my diet" to "improving my health" (combining diet and exercise).

I will now, as an example, demonstrate how I have applied what we have already learned in the previous chapters to my physical health goal.

Make the goal personal: I wish to improve my daily diet to restore my health and the needs of my body, which are terribly weakened due to 8 years of neglect due to the disease gastroparesis and its side-effects. I want to change the quality of food in my diet to more nutrient-dense foods. I want to restore my body's muscle tone and become more active.

Establish your starting point: I recognize that, currently, I have terrible eating habits. Many were created because of gastroparesis. I could not consume foods high in fiber or fat. This restriction did not allow me to consume most proteins, vegetables, or fruits. The illness made me depend almost exclusively on a sugary liquid diet. As a side effect of this poor diet and lack of nutrition, I lost most of my muscle mass. I became weak and debilitated. I hardly have the strength to get up, let alone exercise.

Establish your Destination: My hope is to be able to improve the quality and variety of food I can consume. I will consider my goal achieved when I can eat between five to seven times a day, with smaller but balanced portions filled with nutrients, minerals and vitamins. These foods should also be delicious to my own palate so that I can stick with the changes for a lifetime. I will begin an exercise routine that can be improved little by little. I will consider these goals achieved in stages. The first of which is basic exercises and an improved diet. Eventually to more consistent and difficult exercises with a steady diet (returning to the shape I had before I got sick).

Create SMART goals with action items:

1. Create a diary of food consumed and keep it for a few weeks:
   a. Use a phone app to help keep data from everything consumed in the day.
   b. Add each item to the app after consuming it.
2. Search for foods I like to eat with the nutrients I need:

a. Using the app itself to let me know about the foods I've been consuming to see if it has what I need.

3. Research and replace foods that are not beneficial with alternatives:

a. Make a spreadsheet to classify foods based on personal taste, nutritional value, and cost.

4. Search for companies that offer meal kits to be prepared at home:

a. Search the internet for a company with good prices and a good variety of healthy foods to cook at home.

5. Gradually, replace foods in the diet:

a. Replace at least one food a week with something equivalent but healthier.

6. Schedule time each morning to exercise:

a. Start with 10 minutes a day and, little by little, increase the time and exercises.

b. Take daily walks after lunch or dinner.

Myth: Doing little exercise doesn't work. No pain, no gain.

One of the biggest obstacles many people face is called procrastinating. We often think we must do all or nothing, but the truth is actually the opposite. In my particular case, this was not even an excuse but the reality. I couldn't do more than 10 minutes of exercise a day, even if I wanted to. The point I'm trying to drive home is that we do not need to do too much, but we need to start somewhere and be consistent. To have the discipline to push myself every day was the most important step. Because the initial goal wasn't about getting strong but about forming new habits. I understood that it wasn't a competition, and I stayed focused on improving day by day.

In the same way that dieting only works if we incorporate foods that we like to consume, the habit of exercising will only remain if we do exercises that we enjoy and can improve over time without being driven to extreme exhaustion. In the marathon of your lifetime, don't be the hare; be the turtle.

In the morning, sometimes, even before praying and meditating on scriptures, I would do my 10 minutes of exercises, which began only with stretching. I didn't have the strength to do anything more intense. Still, just stretching provided me with so many benefits. It established wonderful habits that I benefit from to this day. It helped establish the habit of rising early and becoming more alert. Exercise gives you energy and an incredible sense of wellbeing. In the mornings it helped me to fully wake up, and so I prayed more intensely and was more attentive to meditate on the lessons from the Bible.

In the afternoons, I would go for a walk and enjoy the sun on my face and feel the fresh air. I also used this time to talk to friends and family on my mobile. And that was all I needed to get started. Almost immediately, I began to reap the benefits. Science proves that exercising produces endorphins in our brains that generate instant pleasure. In addition, walking and sunbathing improves the health while decreasing stress.

Endorphins have similar properties to morphine and work as a natural pain reliever against body aches. At the end of each walk, I felt happier, more energetic and filled with vitality. At the end of the day, I felt tired, and this helped me to sleep more soundly and be well-rested. The next day, I would wake up ready to do it all over again. This, along with the benefits of eating better, made these decisions easily justified. God created our bodies with a great capacity to repair itself. When you put all the body needs into it, you'll be amazed at how it reacts.

Those were the results of following this plan, but this is where I began. First, I created a list of items I was habitually eating. That list brought to light a negative pattern to the foods I was consuming. The pattern shocked me, as it brought to light knowledge that previously went unnoticed. I was spending an absurd amount of money on foods that were harming me. Another interesting outcome from my analysis was that the healthy foods I began to purchase were costing me less money than the replaced junk food items.

Myth: Healthy foods are too expensive.

Perhaps, a few years ago, this myth may have been true, but as I learned from this experience, I think nowadays the opposite is truer. My research led me to conclude that chips, soda, and candies are more expensive than fruits, vegetables, rice, beans, and most of our staple foods. When I recorded everything my daughter and I were eating, I saw that junk food items are the most expensive, especially when purchased outside the home. Purchases from restaurant chains such as McDonalds and other fast-food competitors quickly add up. In a week, they may end up costing more than a weekly grocery trip would cost to feed your entire family.

In my records, I noted that three trips to McDonalds cost me an average of $54 to feed two people (these estimated calculations were made in the year 2018). Adding the funds spent on coffee from Starbucks and Panera (another similar chain), and I was easily spending over $100 a week. The recordings indicated that I spent $10 per visit for two cups of coffee and $20 if I bought something to eat. Not to mention that these meals were lacking in good nutrition. To make matters worse, I also realized that I was spending at least $30 a week on candy and chocolate. I understood that these habits came out of necessity due to gastroparesis. However, I also understood that it was time to change them. My list was full of non-nutritious foods such as ice cream, cakes, candies, and soda because those were the foods I could eat without getting sick. Now, without the diet restrictions from the illness, it was clearly time to exchange all this "junk" for healthy alternatives.

The purpose of creating the list was accomplished: to bring the problem to light. Now, it's easy to understand where to start. I swapped these foods for fruits (natural sweets), vegetables, almonds, natural juices, and homemade foods. I learned that even though I was buying quality and organic food, I was spending less than before. Instead of eating out at fast food restaurants, I began purchasing food from an online company that delivers fresh ingredients and amazing recipes. I began making homemade meals for about $80 that fed us lunch and dinner every day for a week. In addition to eating well, I benefited from learning how to cook, and the variety of healthy foods has made this habit pleasurable.

Considering that the focus of this book is not on the diet itself, I am using this chapter to leave some practical examples from my personal experience. I did this in the hope that it will encourage you to make some changes as well. Here are a few more:

> 1. I radically cut down my sugar intake by substituting it with honey. When using sugar, I avoid the processed versions and use brown sugar instead.
> 2. I stopped going out to eat and started making homemade meals.
> 3. I replaced soda with natural fruit juices made at home. One of the few items that cost more, but it is well worth it.
> 4. I started drinking lots of water. An overlooked benign and free change

5. I stopped buying coffee at Starbucks and got a top-notch coffee machine. It was an $80 investment, but now I make a delicious cup of coffee with different flavors for only 50 cents on average. In a few months, I've already recouped my investment.

After a few months, I totally changed my diet and eating habits, and the benefits were unbelievable. Vitality returned to my body, and I began to feel full of energy, strength, and vigor. People around me noticed it. I looked and felt healthier.

The compounded benefits I spoke about before spilled over to my exercise routines. One thing affects the other, both on the positive and negative side. If you want to change your life, start with your health because this foundation will affect everything else, including your spiritual life. You will have more strength, disposition and time to serve the Almighty. If you are not healthy, everything is more difficult and, at times, impossible, depending on the gravity of your illness.

So here is my final advice on this topic: Get started today! Don't say to yourself,

— "Today is Thursday; I'm going to start on Monday."

Get started now! It will be worth it. Don't accept excuses because your body and mind will certainly look for them. Take a first step, even if you don't feel like it. If anyone had the right to make excuses, it was me. Gastroparesis left me drained; my body lost a huge amount of muscle mass during these 8 years. At 5'11", I was weighing only 100lbs. I looked and felt like a walking skeleton. But I started doing what I could, and I didn't give up. You can succeed, too. Just get started, and don't give up.

14. Assessing Risks

I built a plan, carried it out by putting it into practice, and even started to see results. Nothing left to worry about, right? Unfortunately, the answer is a resounding no.

Many obstacles will need to be overcome before any goal is reached. Sometimes, these obstacles are so strong and frequent that I can only call them strongholds. These obstacles are unique to each person and, therefore, cannot be all listed or addressed in a book. These are such common human experiences that even scriptures describe them as a reality. They are called spiritual strongholds that manifest in the physical reality. We will discuss them briefly in this chapter, but before we do, I'd like to address a more common variety of issues and risks.

Life is complicated and always changing, but it has patterns. If you identify some of the common risks in life, you can plan to mitigate them before they arise. You can even rank them by impact and likelihood and be ready if they occur. In Project Management, this is called Risk Management, and it's a key part of any project you embark on. In our personal lives, this is no different.

Before you get too anxious about this concept, rest assured that we already do this all the time. We just don't call them Risk Management. Here are some examples:

Any insurance: When you purchase car insurance, you are mitigating or transferring your losses in the event of an accident. You do risk management by considering how much the vehicle is worth, whether you should invest in full coverage or just personal injury protection. You evaluate which policy you can afford and all the options, then decide which contract to acquire. The same concept applies to health insurance or any other type of insurance policy.

Savings: Everyone understands that life can surprise you with some unforeseen events; so ideally, we set aside some money for emergencies. This is another practical example of mitigating risk. Note: if you're living paycheck to paycheck, you may need to make a budget spreadsheet to change this picture (no judgments here. Remember, I was in the same situation a few months ago). I'll talk more about this in a later chapter.

Everyday activities: Looking both ways before you cross the street, stopping at a red light, or taking your daily vitamins are all examples of risk management.

Any activity carried out to prevent, transfer or mitigate the loss of assets due to potential future occurrences is part of risk management. When it comes to our goals and changing habits, the best risk management action we can take is to identify them. If we know them, expect them, and know how to react in advance, we can overcome them. Here are a few I came across and how I dealt with (or still do since these will never really go away in life):

1. Feeling overwhelmed
2. Procrastination
3. Lack of resources
4. Lack of motivation
5. Laziness
6. Negative thoughts and guilt
7. External distractions

I've put them in the order I faced them in my life as I began to document my progress. On occasion, they've over-lapped with one another and still pop up all the time.

I felt completely paralyzed after receiving the healing. As mentioned, my life was completely ruined. I had no idea where to start. Feeling overwhelmed is a common barrier that must be overcome in order to achieve your goals. The best solution to this obstacle is what has already been discussed in previous chapters: identify objectives, rank them, create a plan, and break them down into manageable steps or "SMART" goals. I still think it's worth mentioning this because this obstacle will keep popping up, and we shouldn't allow it to stop us from moving forward. The struggle against it is perpetual.

Procrastination often comes next. Because you are overwhelmed and have no direction, you may keep putting things off. This obstacle is probably one of the biggest and most common. We always say, "I'll start tomorrow" or "we're halfway through the week, I'll start on Monday," but when Monday comes, we postpone it again. My best advice for overcoming this is to start now. Not tomorrow, not the day after, but immediately. Unless you have a restriction that prevents you from acting, do not hesitate. When we start something and see results, we're more likely to keep going and succeed. Even if it's a simple task, like starting a workout routine, take the first step. Start by stretching for ten minutes a day, and eventually, you'll find yourself sticking to a routine and reaping the benefits. Once you've planned, simply get started.

This brings us to the next hurdle: lack of resources. Make sure they're legitimate limitations and that you don't fall under the umbrella of procrastination. For example, if you want to get in shape, then an excuse like "I don't have the money to start a gym membership" is not a legitimate limitation. You don't need equipment, a gym, specific shoes, or any other tool to work out. All you need is time, a routine, and willingness. You can do push-ups, sit-ups, stretches, lunges, squats, and hundreds of other exercises at home at any time. You can go for a walk, jog, and eventually run. You shouldn't have any real reasons not to exercise. The actual limitations will vary depending on your goal or the habit you're trying to change, but make sure they're legitimate. Time and money are the biggest that comes to mind, and both can be managed and overcome, as I have already illustrated.

The lack of motivation is huge. It's another one of those obstacles that comes up frequently and seems to be recurring. Heck, this happens even after we've established habits. If left unchecked, this could be the biggest thorn in your side. My suggestion is to focus on the potential benefits of continuously pursuing your dreams. Visualize the result and celebrate the achievements. Also, reflect on the past and remind yourself of how far you have come. What has worked for me, spiritually speaking, is praising God often. Thank Him by faith for the things to come, and thank Him for being faithful in the past. Hold fast to God's promises and claim, by faith, the victories He assures the obedient through His Word. Of course, motivation looks different for everyone. Find your source of motivation and apply it often.

Laziness is closely linked to a lack of motivation. Your flesh will fight you every step of the way. There will be mornings when you don't want to get up; you will be tempted to take shortcuts; you'll want to skip your workout days. Don't do it! Fight against your will and force yourself to keep going. The beginning can be difficult for some people because humans tend to resist change, but once people begin to see the benefits, they will be less likely to give in to temptations that will derail that success.

For others, danger arises after the habit is established. In the beginning, they are excited and eager to get started, for the dream is still alive in their hearts and minds. However, over time, they start to get bored and experience these urges discussed above. So, get to know yourself and know when you're most likely to have these urges so you can be prepared to overcome them.

Negative thoughts and guilt have been put together because they are usually associated. In most cases, when we make mistakes, fail, or break a routine, we blame ourselves. This can prevent us from continuing, especially when it happens frequently. Every time you fail, you think,

— "I failed, but I'm not going to do it again. I'll be able to do it this time," but then you fail again.

After repeating this cycle of shame and failed attempts, you begin to have negative thoughts about yourself, such as,

— "I'll never make it anyways. I'm a failure so why even try?"

This harsh reality plagues most believers. Guilt is a wall that you build, brick by brick, failure by failure, to the point where you begin to drift away from the Creator. That's the worst thing to do. The best thing is to know that God has provided grace for your mistakes. The love He has for you is independent of what you have done or will do. It is not a license to live in sin, but it is available to every believer. For the non-believer, the truth is much the same: it is necessary to reject defeat. Even knowing that you will likely fail again. Never give up, and understand that this is part of your journey. In both instances, if you get up and improve, you will eventually succeed. Replace negative thoughts with positive ones. Cement this truth in your mind, "Giving up is not an option."

External distractions have a high value in today's digital world. Facebook, Twitter, YouTube, and other social networks can lead us to a monstrous amount of wasted time. Netflix, television, movies, binge-watches, video games, and countless other forms of digital entertainment consume most of people's idle time. And we're not talking about the beneficial kind. I've had to face this problem in my own personal life countless times. They seem to creep up every so often and become progressively worse if not kept in check.

When I finally started to put these lessons into practice and realized that my time was always at a premium, I soon identified the source of the problem. I made the decision that these activities were not worth it. I didn't stop everything at once, but over time, I reduced the number of hours I spent on these external distractions by about 80%. It was hard because the behavior is addictive, so I took the same approach I did when quitting my prescription medication: I walked away a little at a time. Each week, I used these apps and watched television less often. After a few months, it got easier and easier, and as I started to see the benefits, I didn't miss them.

Speaking of external distractions and obstacles, there's one more, and it's the biggest and most often overlooked. I'm going to need to dedicate the entire chapter to do justice to it.

Before I do that, let's discuss the spiritual strongholds I spoke briefly about at the beginning of the chapter. I hope you've noticed by now that these lessons are building upon each other. This particular topic will take us all the way back to chapter 1 – identifying the root of the problem so we can tackle and address it accordingly.

Spiritual strongholds can usually be identified when you do all you can to tackle an issue but find yourself falling in the same areas. A great example would be someone who is an addict. I will use an example that is often shunned but a very real epidemic in our world today: pornography addiction. This issue has become such a monstrous problem of pandemic proportions that it was something that was almost exclusively experienced by men, but today, even women are falling victim to it. The ease of accessibility and lack of public scrutiny have made this a generic worldwide problem. Those who suffer from it usually hide it due to shame. They suffer in silence and solitude.

I say this is a type of spiritual stronghold because the victim becomes enslaved to their own passion and desires. The short-lived pleasure will almost always certainly lead to shame, but the addict feels helpless and bonded by it. This usually results in acceptance (the person surrenders to this destructive force) or oppression resulting by an endless cycle of trying to overcome it alone, followed by the defeat of each attempt. It is destructive and progressive. Like a drug addict, the sensibility erodes over time. The illicit material loses its effect and causes the "user" to seek higher and higher levels of depravity until their very souls feel permanently tainted.

As I mentioned in the previous chapters, this type of stronghold is spiritual. That is why any physical attempt to overcome it often fails. You can try your best to overcome it, but if the problem is spiritual, you will find yourself in a cycle of defeat.

Your resolve will need to be two-fold. First admit it is something beyond your ability to overcome and then seek help, both spiritual and physical.

Physical help may be through a trusted friend or mentor. Someone who will help you and keep you accountable until you overcome this bondage. It will be very difficult and, again, perhaps even impossible without tackling the spiritual side. The side you can only overcome through Christ and faith, but not blind faith. The biblical faith is called Emunah. Faith through action.

"For though we live in the world, we do not wage war as the world does. The weapons we fight with are not the weapons of the world. On the contrary, they have divine power to demolish strongholds" 2 Corinthians 10:3,4 (NIV)

That can be achieved when you seek the Lord for help and ask for understanding. Ask God to help you see people through His eyes and transform your way of thinking (your mind) by applying biblical principles in your life.

"Do not conform to the pattern of this world, but be transformed by the renewing of your mind." Romans 12:2a (NIV)

15. Secret Enemies

A jealous and malicious person may pretend to be an ally while secretly sabotaging our accomplishments and goals. These are the most dangerous enemies, as we are often not aware of their intentions until it is too late. It is a tragedy that repeats itself and which, if neglected, could be our undoing. I'll provide an illustration:

In the tenth season of AMC's much-watched TV show "The Walking Dead," a new group of enemies has emerged. After five years of considerable peace among the surviving communities that faced extreme situations in a zombie apocalypse, society is facing a new threat: the Whisperers. They are so-called because they live among the dead, guiding them for their own benefit. They wear leather masks made from the deceased and do not utter a single word as they walk among the dead, except for a few whispers from select members when the group needs to be redirected or instructed. Please track with me and remember that I am describing a fictional show. I am just laying the groundwork for using this show's plot to illustrate my point.

After some direct confrontations between the groups that led to the deaths of several characters, the leader of the Whisperers, Alpha, used a common war strategy: she sent a spy to Alexandria. Alexandria is the community of the protagonists of the show. In doing so, she devised a plan that would perhaps lead to their self-destruction from the inside out. Dante was chosen for the task and executed it perfectly by infiltrating the community. He joined a random group of strangers who, at some point, joined the community in Alexandria. Once inside, Dante befriended the community doctor, Siddiq, and eventually wreaked havoc. He caused many members of the community to turn against each other; used propaganda through graffiti that caused suspicion in already fragile relationships; sabotaged the water supply, causing many to become sick; And he even killed some patients with his bare hands, the very people he was supposed to be helping. He was ruthless, calculating, and malicious, doing all of this under the guise of being benevolent and a good friend. In the end, Siddiq discovered who he really was because of a traumatic event that brought his memories of Dante back, however, it was too late. Once Dante realized that Siddiq had figured out his plot, he eliminated Siddiq. The damage had already been done.

Dante is a perfect example of what an unknown or hidden enemy can do. A formidable enemy that you can see and fight head-on is dangerous but manageable. However, an enemy that operates behind the scenes or in the shadows is a much bigger and probably deadly threat. An enemy that pretends to be a friend is the most challenging you can face. Regardless of whether you believe or are aware of it, we have such an enemy. And he's ready to destroy you.

There's something common to every conspiracy theory you've ever heard of. All of them, whether plausible or not, use this terminology:

— "They are hiding the truth from us"; "They're lying"; "They're poisoning our food"; "They this..."; "They that..."; "They, they, they..."

Nevertheless, if you ask the people who believe in these theories who "they" are, there will be no clear answer. Or the answers will vary between aliens, the elite, the Illuminati, the government, reptilian beings, or a combination of all of these. Before you attack the conspiracy theorists, remember that they are not all on the same level. Some are a bit weird (to be polite). However, there are some conspiracy theories that are no longer theories. The government has publicized some conspiracies as events that have happened.

An example is the mind control experiments conducted by the CIA on the general population and on an unauthorized controlled group. I'm talking about MK Ultra, a now documented historical fact. A decade ago, it was true only in the minds of a few "crazy" conspiracy theorists. That's just one example.

So far in this book, I have brought up some examples of Christians who hold the extreme view that everything is spiritual. Most of them neglect physical reality. Now, I'll do the opposite. After all, we're focusing on finding a balanced life in this book. We have already talked about how many physical manifestations of illness or problems can arise from emotional issues, but they can also originate in the spirit or spiritual realm. The Bible says that "our battle is not against flesh and blood, but against rulers and authorities, against the powers of this world of darkness and against the spiritual forces of evil in the heavenly places," in Paul's letter to the Ephesians, chapter 6. The "they" common to all conspiracy theories, in my opinion, are "fallen angels" or "demons." The spiritual forces are described in the verse above. They are very real and consistently plotting against humanity in order to profane God.

The chief of the fallen angels is known by many names and has many titles. Some have called him Satan, Lucifer, the devil, the ancient serpent, the dragon, among many others. This entity presents two equally deadly proposals to humanity: the first is that he is the liberator of humanity from a tyrannical and malevolent God who has kept us as slaves with false promises and lies. The second is simply that he doesn't exist. He's honed his craft over millennia, but his tactics have been the same since the Garden, and he continues to use them for a single solitary reason: they work.

It is important to be aware of his existence, but it's even more important to know how he attacks us and why. That is the only way we can defend ourselves when facing such evil. Most likely, you will never meet this entity in person, as he is not omnipresent like the Creator. However, he controls a network of fallen angels and demons who act as a false copy of this power of God.

You see, the first thing you should know about our enemy is that he is a liar and cannot create anything as God can. Therefore, he is limited by what has been created. He alters God's original creation to suit his needs. His goal is to mock the Creator or to dishonor Him. He hates the Lord and, therefore, hates us, the creatures created in the image and likeness of God. I'll be practical and won't go into too much detail. It would be impossible to share everything revealed in scripture or known principles about this enemy. As a result, I'll once again summarize a few key points:

> 1. He's real, though he thrives on making people believe that he's not.
> 2. He's a big threat but often presents as if he's not.
> 3. He wants to destroy your life and everything that represents God.
> 4. He is a liar and a deceiver and appears as an angel of light.
> 5. He is in control of this world and its system.

I'll start with the last point because it's the least obvious. How can the devil be in control of this world, and at the same time, God, the Creator, be Omnipotent? Simple, God has set rules and is righteous, so He cannot go against them. When

God created the world, He gave Adam and Eve all dominion over it, giving them free will to do whatever they wanted with it. The only rule that God established was not to eat the fruit of the tree of the knowledge of good and evil. However, that is an irrelevant topic for this discussion. The relevance lies in the fact that Satan, the ancient serpent, tempted Eve and made her disobey God. Thus, he assumed the authority over the domain that was given to mankind.

Adam and Eve surrendered their authority by obeying the serpent's voice and were separated from the Creator, becoming spiritually dead, as God had warned them about. Satan became the new ruler of the world and continues to be to this day. If that wasn't true, then he couldn't have offered Jesus, God incarnate, all the kingdoms of the world when He tempted Him in the wilderness.

"Again, the devil took him to a very high mountain and showed him all the kingdoms of the world and their splendor. 'All this I will give you,' he said, 'if you will bow down and worship me.'" Matthew 4:8,9 (NIV)

Satan could not have offered Jesus anything that was not his, especially to the Son of God.

Be aware. Satan has power, but he is limited, and because he is not omniscient like God, he can only plan to a certain extent without knowing God's ultimate plan. If he had known, he would never have crucified Jesus. What Satan believed to be his greatest victory turned out to be his greatest downfall.

At the end of all times, the same will happen. God will judge everyone by complying with His own rules, denying no one free will but still claiming a decisive victory. Until that happens, you need to know that Satan is the ruler of the present world system and that we have authority over him if we do what God wants.

When we disobey God, we give Satan and his minions authority over us, and that's when they do their best to destroy us. It's a simplified version of the spiritual warfare we face, whether we're aware of it or not. The truth is that if you don't pose a threat to Satan's system, you're likely to be less targeted than if you're making a difference in God's Kingdom.

If you belong to Christ and you don't understand what I'm saying, then you're probably in an even worse position than an unbeliever. It means that you're not a threat to the enemy or doing much for the Kingdom of God. I don't say this in a judgmental tone because I've been in that situation before, but it's something that you need to think about. Perhaps it is time to take a stand and start seeking God's will for your life.

This topic may seem irrelevant and out of place when compared to the other chapters. However, I assure you it is an integral part of achieving a balanced and fulfilled life. Believe it or not, this spiritual battle is happening all around you. As a believer, you may be bombarded by these entities. Being controlled or influenced by these evil forces, even if you are not aware of them. Look for patterns in life, and you'll start to see what I'm trying to expose. If something abnormal happens once, it may be random. If it happens two or three times, surely, it's a strange coincidence. However, if it happens more often than that, you should probably start questioning the reason and take a closer look. Whenever you start having "weird coincidences" in your life, pay attention. I can't tell you exactly what to look for, but I've given you some examples that I've seen in my life during this phase. The voice within me when I contemplated suicide. The voice that burned within me during the movie "Frozen 2". The voice I constantly heard when seeking employment. These are just a few examples of how the Spirit truly speaks and guides us. I will share a bit more insight into how this occurs.

When believers say that God speaks to them daily, most people begin to question their sanity. They probably think they hear audible voices, and anyone who hears voices in their head needs to be hospitalized or medicated. I don't think that's how God speaks, although He can. But in general, He guides us through signs, His Spirit, and His written Word. Signs can include daily circumstances, people (He can use anyone, inside or outside the church), our memories, visions, and dreams, among countless others.

Often, when I'm facing a specific problem or challenge in life, He uses many of these ways to guide me. I can't explain how, but I know in my heart and spirit that the instruction came from Him. In decades of following God, this has happened to me in so many unexpected ways. As I noted before, if it had happened once, I'd say it was random. If it had happened two or three times, it would probably have been a coincidence. Yet it has happened so often, in different ways, always with wonderful clarity and results, that I am convinced that it is indeed the Almighty God speaking to me. As unworthy as I am and as unfathomable as it may seem, the Creator of the universe speaks to this insignificant person. It would be easier to convince myself that my wife does not exist than to convince myself of the nonexistence or impersonality of God. Obviously, I know my wife is real, but my point is that my relationship with God is just as tangible as my most intimate relationship on earth.

Therefore, if God is real and what He says is true, then the devil is also real and should be taken seriously, as the Scriptures tell us. With that said, I don't believe we should fear him; just be aware of his wiles so that we can stand firm when he or his subordinates attack us.

Fact: You can learn valuable lessons from the devil.

It's also fascinating that we can learn from this foe. In my life, since my youth, I have tried to learn from the mistakes of others. Fearing facing the same consequences, I observe people and avoid the same pitfalls. The same can be said about this adversary.

One lesson you can learn from Satan is that he is legalistic. That is, he is aware of our rights and that he must first take away our authority before he does anything against us. This is true even for those who do not know or follow Christ. You can ask any Satanist or occult follower if you know any, and they will confirm this established rule. Their books and publications confirm this. No evil can be done without consent, even if it is gained by trickery. Even if you hear people talking about the Illuminati or members of secret societies, they will tell you that these people put their message out in the open, through symbolism or occult messages, to get the public's consent before they do their evil deeds or rituals. These people are guided by spiritual beings and demonic entities and are instructed to follow these rules. They know that they need to follow the rules set by God before they can do any work.

You have authority over them and your life, so the only way they can act against you is if you let them. When you give in to temptation and sin, you are, in a sense, giving them authority to rule over you. Again, ignorance does not change reality. For example, if you break a law that you are not aware of and are taken to court, the judge will never accept your excuse for not knowing the law and will sentence you accordingly. A good and compassionate judge may take this into account and lower your sentence or give you a warning if the crime is not serious, but in order to do proper justice, the judge is bound by the law.

Another lesson is that he wants to appear bigger than he

really is. If Satan fails to make you believe he's not real, his next best strategy is to befriend you or get you to fear him. Either way, he wants to look grander than he really is. By befriending you, he will do what he did to Eve. He will tell you that God is your true enemy and that He is hiding things from you.

He said to Eve:

"You will certainly not die. For God knows that in the day you eat of it, your eyes will be opened, and like God, you will know good and evil." Genesis 3:4,5 (NIV)

That was the oldest lie ever told. First, he made God look like the real liar by telling Eve that she would not die. Next, he made God the villain who was somehow hiding things from His creation, saying,

— "God knows that if you eat, you will be like Him."

The saddest part of this lie is that Eve already had eternal life and access to all the knowledge she could ever desire; she had access to the Creator God.

Even today, we fall for this lie all the time. Humanity has been trying to regain what has been lost since the fall. We always try to return to our original state: eternal life and access to all knowledge. Satan still makes these false promises. He pretends to be Lucifer, the light-bearer who brings forbidden and hidden knowledge to those who seek him. All these secret societies are centered on Lucifer worship. "Light" worship. Sun worship. Some are just more open about it than others.

The other way he tries to appear bigger is through fear. If he can't be invisible or look like an ally, he tries to present himself as invincible. He walks "like" a roaring lion, looking for someone to devour. Scripture describes him "as" a roaring lion, for he is not a lion. He even tries to show himself on an equal footing with God, but he is far from it. The Bible says that Jesus is the Lion of Judah. So, Satan tries to show himself to be as powerful as God, but no matter how much he may roar, he will never be a lion. In comparison, he's not even a kitten. Don't think I'm underestimating him. He is our greatest and most dangerous adversary, but God is infinitely more powerful. The devil has power, but the Lord is all-powerful.

The last lesson I want to share is that Satan is an accuser. He loves to accuse God's children and try to make us feel guilty and unworthy of divine love. He reminds us of our past and present sins and tries to draw us away from the Creator. He is a master at making us feel like we can't get close to God because of our flaws. But as Christians, we have an advocate who pleads our case before the Father: Jesus Christ, who washed us from our sins and clothed us with His righteousness. No matter what Satan says or accuses, we cannot be separated from God's love in Christ Jesus. He accepts us as we are and loves us unconditionally. There is no condemnation for those who are in Christ Jesus.

These are just a few of the strategies Satan uses against us. It is important for us to be aware of these tactics so that we can resist the devil and remain steadfast in our faith. That is why the Bible instructs us to be vigilant and put on the full armor of God to resist the wiles of the devil. Remember that the ultimate victory has already been won by Jesus on the cross, and we have the power and authority to resist the enemy and live an abundant life in Christ.

There is one more thing worth sharing about the devil, and by observing his history and behavior, pride always precedes a fall.

The devil was a creation of God and was perfect, but because of the pride that grew in his heart, he came to see himself as superior to God. Similarly, when we begin to achieve some of our goals, we are tempted to feel proud. Our carnal nature is contrary to our spirit and, if left unchecked, will lead us to fall. Remind yourself often of how you got to where you are and where you've been. Always remain humble.

16. Balanced Budget

E very four years, during the U.S. election for the prestigious office of the President, candidates from both parties discuss ways to improve the country's gross domestic product (GDP) and achieve a balanced budget. This has not happened since 2001, when the budget was in financial surplus. Since then, this nation has entered a spiral of increasing debt. Every year, Americans spend more than they earn. I believe that the current state of the country reflects the state of its citizens. Most are sinking into debt, living paycheck to paycheck beyond their means, and on the verge of bankruptcy.

I was in the same situation, so to speak. Due to conditions beyond my control and perhaps something you can all relate to I had lost control of my finances. Diseases are costly. Our country has failed us when it comes to adequate and afford-able medical care. I had health insurance, a job, substantial savings, and everything anyone could have to prevent this from happening, but it still happened. Being sick for almost a decade is very expensive, and that's what I experienced. However, I don't want to focus on how or why I got to this position but rather on how I changed my situation through God, a plan, and actions. You may find yourself in a similar situation in different circumstances, but you too can take steps to take back control and come out on top. Like me, don't focus on why you got there or try to blame others. Instead, take control of the situation and devise a plan for self-liberation.

Myth: Money is the root of all evil.

This myth comes from one of the most misunderstood

biblical verses. The Bible says that the "love" of money is the root of "many" evils. In addition to being healthy and having good relationships with others, the next area that needs to be addressed is financial stability. It's naïve to think and say that money isn't important. Many unhinged believers may think or say this, but in our current reality and in this world system, almost everything depends on money. If money or possessions were not important, then the bible wouldn't address it over 800 times.

Jesus' parables talked about money or wealth 11 out of 40 times. That's more than 25% of his parables. If the Bible talks a lot about money, then I won't hesitate to devote a large chapter to address it. Jesus often talked about money because it often reveals people's hearts and intent. That is why the love of money is the root of many problems. Here are a few things Jesus said about money:

"No one can serve two masters. Either you will hate the one and love the other, or you will be devoted to the one and despise the other. You cannot serve both God and money." Matthew 6:24 (NIV)

"...So, give back to Caesar what is Caesar's, and to God what is God's." Matthew 22:21b (NIV)

The Bible also talks about a type of debt-based slavery or servitude:

"The rich rule over the poor, and the borrower is slave to the lender" Proverbs 22:7 (NIV)

Jesus illustrates this in His parables about a creditor and a debtor,

"As he began the settlement, a man who owed him ten thousand bags of gold was brought to him. Since he was not

able to pay, the master ordered that he and his wife and his children and all that he had be sold to repay the debt." Matthew 18:24,25 (NIV)

What a revolting revelation! If we understand this correctly, all of us, or almost all of us, are slaves. In fact, we are slaves to the system of this world and remember, Satan is the current owner and administrator of this system. Isn't it ironic that, believer or not, we often hear and use words like,

— "The system is rigged."

or

— "I feel like the system is designed to be against me?"

That's because it's true. After I understood this, I quickly decided to start plotting my own deliverance. With God's help, I was able to achieve it.

First, transform your mind (change your mental conditioning). We grew up in this world, and because of that, we mirror its mentality. We think that debt is a normal part of life and that it is inevitable, but Satan and his workers cannot have authority over us unless we grant it. Remember, he's a legalist.

I've listed below some actions you may need to adopt before you begin (at a minimum, be aware of them and ponder to see if they will add value to your life):

> 1. Don't buy anything without thinking about it for a long period. The larger and more significant the purchase, the longer you should consider.
> 2. If you decide to buy something, save money for it and buy it in cash.
> 3. Reprioritize your needs over your wants.

4. Make investments instead of purchases.

5. Learn the system and use it to your advantage instead of being undermined by it.

6. Use credit cards only for their convenience and benefits. Do not use it if you cannot pay the balance at the end of the month. Avoid interest.

7. Make and stick to a budget.

The first six are more concepts and states of mind that you should have when dealing with money. The last one, the dreaded budget, is the most practical and is where we all need to start our journey. Without a budget or plan, you will surely fail. Remember the rules for each goal?

1. Make it personal.

2. Know where you're starting.

3. Know when you've reached your goal or objective.

Well, you can't do the second one without a budget. So that's where I started, and that's where you should also start if you don't already have it ready.

Shall we practice what we have already learned? Start with SMART goals and with specific actions:

1. Create a budget:
   a. Use Excel or an app to list all your monthly expenses. (I used an Excel template to get started and then found an app called Credit Karma on the Internet.)
   b. Use bank statements for the last three months to list all your transactions and purchases and put them in the correct category.

c. Assess your spending habits and identify where you can reduce and make changes or substitutions.

d. Make sure your income is enough to pay for all monthly expenses with a minimum of 25% to spare (i.e., all your bills and expenses should only add up to 75% of your income. If not, you need to reduce expenses or increase your income).

e. Apply the surplus.

   i. At least 10% of this surplus should be saved if you have debt. The remaining 15% should be used to pay off your debts as soon as possible.

   ii. If you don't have debt, the entire 25% should be saved.

Note: Savings can also be subdivided for planned future purposes, such as a vehicle or a family trip. Saving doesn't just mean having money you don't touch (although I'd still suggest that 10% is that kind of saving).

This plan is a simplified version of a budget template. Again, this book isn't about finances or budgeting, so you'll need to research more about what to do in your situation. I'm showing you just a little bit of what I've done. For the sake of practicality, I'll give you just a few examples of what's happened in my life and how I've made decisions that have helped me overcome difficulties in this area. Keep in mind that all these tidbits and examples serve to expose principles. They are not just page fillers. They serve a purpose to those attentive enough to perceive them.

Like my assessment portion for my "getting healthy" goals, I was incredulous to see how and where our money was being spent. Here are a few things that caught my eye and what I did about it:

Subscriptions: We all have the mindset that if an item only costs $1, $2, or even $5, it doesn't make a difference. However, these values add up. I noticed that every month, we were spending over $100 on different subscriptions. Some that I had forgotten about and was paying every month without my knowledge. Items my daughter signed up for on the iPhone because the apps were "free" to download, but they had a hidden agreement that after a certain trial period, they would charge us monthly. Some were subscriptions that I no longer used but never canceled. These bills were causing our bank balance to bleed. Without the budget or monitoring our spending, I would never have realized this. After modifications were made, I only kept a $9.99 Microsoft subscription for software I use often, a Netflix subscription for $9.99, and an Xbox subscription for $4.99 that my daughter uses for entertainment. A significant difference. Now, that $75 difference can be saved or applied elsewhere. NOTE: I called many of the apps that were billing me monthly and demanded a refund. Most of them agreed since I hadn't accessed their system in years, so I got a good refund. It's worth a try.

Eating out and coffee: I mentioned this in the chapter on eating healthier, but it's worth mentioning again. Food expenses, such as eating out along and weekly grocery shopping, were between $600 to $800 per month (back in 2018). Simply absurd. Over the months, I replaced eating out with eating healthy at home and started buying items I used frequently in bulk. Now, I spend only about half the amount on food items and we're eating much healthier than before.

Entertainment: When you have a child, entertainment expenses are a part of life. We take our daughter out often. Even when we were sick, she would go out with her grandmother or other people, but we always paid the bill. As a result, expenses for the zoo, skating park, aquarium, gymnastics, dancing, shopping, movies, and other activities piled up. This remains inevitable, but planning makes a big difference. For example, there's an app called Groupon that shows different promotions offered by different locations. We recently went to the zoo for $1 each, which would normally cost $12 each. AT&T offers a "buy one, get one free" movie ticket for Tuesday nights. Different options like that. Another hack, and please don't judge, is to pack healthy food and snacks when you go out. It's healthier anyway, and food is one of the biggest expenses when going out. A movie, for example, costs about $10 per person, depending on the time and place. However, when you add popcorn, soda, candy, and other goodies, you can easily spend $50 on a movie night. The same candy they sell for $5 costs about $1 at the grocery store. So why spend $50 when you can spend $20 for the same experience? Don't be proud, and don't give in to the pressures of the world. Be humble as doves but wise as serpents. I haven't decreased the frequency of entertainment activities, but I spend about a third of what I used to.

Phone, cable TV, and internet: I was shocked when I saw my AT&T and Cox bills added together. I realized that these three bills added up to more than my rent. Without a doubt, your mortgage or rent should always be your biggest expense. If anything comes close to that, you're overpaying. These companies take advantage of people by offering great packages at the beginning and slowly increasing them over the years. My wife used to keep an eye on these things, but with her illness, that too went unnoticed. I acted quickly and called them. Ultimately, I was able to cancel Cox and consolidate all three accounts with AT&T, reducing the amount to a third of what I was originally paying. Also, I got faster internet and better TV channels. I'm in no way endorsing the company.

111

It happened to be the best option available to me at the time, and because of my work, we had an additional 20% off the bill, so for me, it turned out to be the best offer. Research the local suppliers available in your area and know that, as a consumer, you have the power to negotiate.

Budgeting was an eye-opening experience. Without doing the budget, none of these necessary changes would have been evident. It took a lot of work and adjustments in the first few months and required daily monitoring to ensure that actions were being done correctly. Now, all of this requires minimal effort.

Today, I don't even require daily checks. I know every penny that comes out of my account and where it goes, so any transaction that is out of the ordinary catches my eye. I have my Mint app set on autopilot. All my accounts, cards, and investments are linked to this phenomenal free app. Since they're part of TurboTax and QuickBooks, doing my taxes every year was a breeze.

Regarding my list at the beginning of the chapter, some of these points may seem obvious, but I want to give examples so that you may apply these concepts in your life. That is why I made the disclaimer at the beginning of the book. I warned you that I would go into meticulous detail because I don't know each reader's knowledge level. Maybe the section about diet was new to you but obvious to others, and the opposite is happening here. Please use the examples to enforce things you already know and to learn things you may not know. Here we go:

Item 1 – thinking about big purchases. This lesson should be taken very seriously. If you recall my original goals list in the earlier chapters, you will recall that I labeled buying a new car as a "foolish pursuit." A car obviously qualifies as a big-ticket item. Most people, me included, would quickly justify this purchase by saying,

— "Everyone needs a car, and almost everyone has a car loan. It's just part of life."

Myth: Living with debt is inevitable in today's economy

The reality is that this simply isn't, and doesn't have to be, true in anyone's life. This epiphany led me to eventually change my mind about the purchase. After pondering and considering this goal, I decided it wasn't worth adding an unnecessary burden and expense to my life. My car was having mechanical issues at the time, and that was one of the reasons I was considering buying a new one. That and the fact that I, like most men, can't resist the temptation to have a shiny new toy. My car was having its battery continuously drained. I replaced it once, thinking it would solve the problem. It lasted a few months, but then it happened again and left me stranded. This frustration is what led me to the desire to replace the vehicle. Like most people these days, I just wanted a quick fix and wasn't interested in finding what was causing the battery to fail. I just wanted the problem gone.

Now, with the new mindset, I took the vehicle to the mechanic. They were able to finally diagnose the source. It was a faulty alternator[2]. The dealership wanted to charge me $1,800 to replace this part. An outside mechanic, a friend of my father-in-law's, offered me to do the same job for $1,200. Both were way over my budget at the time (this was still when I was unemployed and receiving unemployment benefits). I prayed and asked God for wisdom and a solution. I needed a car and simply didn't have that amount of cash available.

---

2 For those who don't have mechanical knowledge, this is a part of the vehicle that is directly connected to the engine by a belt, and as the car runs, the rotation produces an electrical voltage that powers the car's electronics while recharging the car's battery.

On the same day, while watching YouTube, one of the videos that popped up on my feed was about a mechanic fixing his Toyota in his driveway and offering a free tutorial. This piqued my interest because my car is a 2008 Toyota Highlander. I'm not kidding... he was replacing the alternator on his 2010 Toyota Highlander. Another one of those "coincidences" I spoke of before. It seemed difficult, and the YouTuber mentioned that it wasn't an easy job. As I watched the video, I gained confidence. The next day, I researched the price of the alternator in several stores and found a local supplier who offered it for $238. Since I had more time than money, I decided to give it a try. It wasn't easy. It took me all day to get the job done, but the sense of accomplishment and satisfaction at the end of a long day was almost intoxicating. I did it. An added surprise was that I was able to return the old part and get a $50 refund. My car was running smoothly, and I spent $1,000 less than my lowest estimated bid. The lesson here is that every situation has a workaround. Search for it, and you'll find it.

The other lesson is related to thinking outside of the box. Consider every potential option before committing to long-term debt or high-value purchases. And have the confidence to try something you've never done before. Take calculated risks.

Items 2 and 3 – Saving and prioritizing. When you decide you need something, save up for it. Even a car. The only exclusion would be your mortgage for your primary residence or an investment property. Still, if you can, save as much as you can and pay off the loan as soon as possible. A car would be the second consideration, but even a vehicle can be purchased outright. If you really need a car right away, then buy a used vehicle in good condition. Research and find one for a good price and, yes, save up to buy it outright. Cash purchases give you the power to negotiate and get better deals.

Even better, you can avoid paying interest. Make sure your purchase is based on a need and not a desire. Maybe you want the latest Xbox, but you don't need that. If you wait a few months, you can save money and probably pay a fraction of the price by buying it used from someone else. I've seen people even go so far as to overpay for items they want immediately. I have a perfect real-life example:

In 2006, I stood in line on Black Friday to buy the Nintendo Wii and PS3 when they were first released. These were things I wanted at the time, so I woke up at 3 a.m. and stood out in the cold with many other people to make sure I was able to purchase it. Since they were sold out everywhere and people wanted to buy them for Christmas, they were selling for a ridiculous amount on eBay that year. I decided to put my desires aside and listed them, thinking I could make some extra money that year and buy my own devices the following year. I was shocked when each of them sold for about 10 times what I paid. It shows people's desperation to get what they want instead of what they need. This emphasizes that the lack of self-control or patience to wait can become very costly.

Item 4 - Make investments rather than purchases. I've already given a few examples of this when I talked about buying the K-Latte coffee machine. That wasn't a purchase. It was an investment. I paid $80 upfront for an item that I honestly didn't need. I purchased it because I knew I would keep buying coffee for $5 a cup at Starbucks if I didn't buy the machine. I made an investment that paid for itself in about a month. Within the first month, I recouped the investment amount. The ROI (Return on Investment) was easily calculated before the decision to make the purchase was established and eventually concluded. Since then, I've been saving money while continuing to enjoy the benefits.

I read a book about finance a long time ago. Unfortunately, I don't remember the name of the book or the author (I believe it was "Rich Dad Poor Dad" by Robert Kiyosaki and Sharon Lechter), but something the author wrote stuck in my mind ever since:

— "Don't buy what you want. Instead, buy assets that will make a profit for you and let those assets buy what you want." (Paraphrased)

That surprised me. It was a book about investing in real estate and he was talking about delayed gratification. He said,

— "Maybe you want to buy a flat-screen TV that costs $5,000 today, but instead, save the $5,000 and put it toward a rental property purchase. Eventually, you'll own a property that pays enough passive income to pay for at least 5 flat-screen TVs a year." (Paraphrased)

That made perfect sense to me. If you make smart investments and think long-term, you'll be able to enjoy better things without having to spend your hard-earned money. It's a difficult concept to illustrate, but it makes sense. That's how millionaires and billionaires live. They live off the interest earned. They have all their money and property generating accumulated passive income for them, so the money they spend is earned without work. The assets work for them. I tested this theory with a video game. I set up two accounts in the same game called Raid Shadow Legends. In this game, you have the option to invest your gems in a gem mine (gems are the items in the game that cost real money to obtain and help you increase your progress with less effort). The gem mine costs 1,500 gems and produces only 15 gems per day. At first, you may think,

— "If I buy this mine, it will take 100 days to get my gems back (ROI), and I need to invest those gems in other in-game resources to unlock them. I can always buy the mine later when I've got the resources; I need to progress through the game now."

However, to my surprise, after three months of play (the hundred days calculated for the ROI), I noticed that the account with the mine was better off. The account I invested in the mine, I was able to unlock all the other resources with the gems produced by the mine, the 15 gems per day, and I still had 1,875 gems left. The other account, where I didn't buy the mine, didn't have all the available resources unlocked yet, and I only had 75 gems saved. How? That doesn't make sense. It does, and I'll explain how.

The account I invested in the mine grew a bit slower at first, but as I used the daily gems to unlock other resources, they gave me compounding benefits. These resources also produced some additional gems. After the first month, the accounts were evenly matched, more or less equal. However, from that point on, the account with the mine grew exponentially, while the account without the mine continued to grow at the same steady fixed rate. After only three months, it was very clear which choice was better.

Life works a bit like this video game. You can get what you want now and keep growing at a steady rate, or you can sacrifice a little, invest now, and then experience exponential growth. Thus, you will be able to get everything you need and want without jeopardizing your financial stability or future.

Learn how the system works and use it to your advantage. This includes many things I've already mentioned. Money has bargaining and purchasing power. Buy used items in similar condition to new counterparts. Don't go and purchase them new from a retail store, especially electronics. Plan your purchases and wait for promotions. Buy quality items at a frac-

117

tion of the cost. I'll give you some examples of purchases I made early in my journey.

I'll start by describing my first purchase after I got a job. However, before I talk about that, I must take a moment to glorify God. After providing every financial need for over a year, He opened the best possible opportunity. It was a dream job with an excellent company called Hexagon. Best of all, this opportunity allowed me to work from home. This was essential for my current situation. I had a sick wife and a young daughter. It was in itself an indispensable benefit for me. However, it required me to have a dedicated location at home to comply with the company's rules, which is why I needed to set up a home office. A place where I could work, be productive, and not be interrupted. Because I didn't want to violate my own first and second rules, I took my time before making any purchases. I realized it was a major expense because I needed a desk and an ergonomic office chair. I didn't want to just go to an office furniture store and spend thousands of dollars on quality office furniture. Instead, I worked with what I had while applying my recently learned principles.

In the first month, I set up all the work equipment on my kitchen countertop. The only investment I made was to buy a used stool for $5 at a garage sale. I began to save money and kept my eyes open for deals on the internet. I established a $500 budget allocated for this purpose and kept saving up cash until the moment of purchase. I searched daily on a Facebook group I joined, which connects local people who are selling their belongings. It's a bit like Craig's List, only more localized, and all members are verified. Every time a piece of furniture caught my eye, I would contact the seller and arrange a visit. Generally, they were too small, were in terrible shape, or were too expensive. I started to think that I'd probably have to save more or settle for something of lower quality. I opted to keep saving because I knew this would be a purchase I would use for a long time. The quality would be an essential prerequisite.

About a week later, the opportunity presented itself. The photos on the listing looked too good to be true. So, I acted quickly because the seller advertised them for only $400. The following day, I visited the seller's house, and the furniture was indeed as good as they were advertised. I made the purchase. In the end, with delivery included the unit cost $525. A bit over my planned budget, but it included a leather chair that was practically new. They were the sole owners and took very good care of the items. The best part came later. I searched for the same exact furniture online to see if I got a good deal. I couldn't believe it. The same furniture, if bought new, would cost $3,500 (excluding the chair). These models are usually sold directly to large companies and are marketed only through catalogs.

Applying the principles of saving first, paying cash, buying used, and waiting for the right opportunity saved me about 80% of the retail value. I applied the same principles with many other items I wanted. Some I even bought impulsively because the opportunity presented itself. Now that I have the means and available disposable cash when a great offer comes along, I can make the most of the opportunity.

Lastly, and with that, I believe the topic has been exhausted for this book; I leave you with a cardinal rule: use credit cards, but don't let credit cards use you. One of the reasons I mentioned in the budget section that you should use the 15% surplus money to pay off your debts is because of the interest. It doesn't make sense to put that 15% surplus money into a savings account where it's going to earn interest of 0.1-2% per year when you have debt that charges interest of 6-18% per year. It's simple math: If you put $1,000 into a savings account and receive interest of 0.1% per month (the national average), you'll earn only $2 in interest a month. However, if you owe $1,000 on a credit card that charges interest of 12% per year (which is below the national average), you'll have an additional $10 in debt at the end of the month (Note: APR stands for Annual Percentage Rate, so you multiply the percentage by the balance and divide it by 12 to get the monthly interest. In this example, 12% of $1,000 is $120, so the monthly interest is $120/12 or $10). You can quickly see why it's a better investment to direct that money toward minimizing debt rather than putting it into savings. It's wise to quickly pay off all those debts first before putting extra money into savings. This goes for the use of credit cards in general. Always pay off your balance at the end of the month.

If you buy something with credit, it simply means that you bought something you can't afford. I still believe that credit cards can be used to your advantage, with benefits like improving your credit score and getting benefits on the money you'll spend anyway. Some examples include frequent flyer miles, cash back, and other rewards. If you're going to spend the money anyway, why not get the benefits before you pay off the card? Use the cards, but don't let them use you.

Here are a few more brief tips:

1. Consolidate debts with lower interest rates. If you have a lot of cards with different balances and interest rates, think about getting a larger line of credit with lower interest rates and consolidating them.
2. Improve your credit score to get better deals. You can now get your credit score for free. The app I suggested earlier, Mint, monitors your credit and helps you improve it for free. My credit score went from about 400 (horrible)

to about 600 (fair) in three months and keeps going up. I am now receiving offers from lenders to reduce interest rates on existing loans. (**Note**: Today, in 2024, my credit is over 800 (excellent) as a testimony that you can do it with effort and discipline).

3. Call creditors and try to negotiate agreements. Lenders know that people can't repay loans if they go bankrupt. Call them and try to negotiate the repayment of large debts for a fraction of the amount owed. I've negotiated payments of only 10% of what I owed. Don't feel bad; these mega-corporations and banks have already made this money from you ten times, and they know it. Be fair and be prepared to pay for your mistakes, but there's nothing wrong with asking, and you'll be surprised at the results.

With all that said, I'm still far from where I'd like to be financially, but by the grace of God, I've pulled out of a deep hole and am now comfortably above ground. I know it's just the beginning. You can get to that position too.

People are so used to living paycheck to paycheck that they can't see past the next week. Don't think like that. Work hard now, save, and invest, and in due time, you'll be able to enjoy the financial freedom you crave.

Finally, item 5 talks about learning how the system works so you can use it to your advantage. Believers tend to have a negative mindset toward the system. The truth is that the system isn't necessarily bad; it's just a set of rules and principles that govern society. If you don't understand the rules and play accordingly, you'll be beaten. However, if you learn them, know how to play the game and use the loopholes to your advantage, you can succeed within the system. This is true in all aspects of life, including finances. For example, the tax system is a set of rules that governs how taxes are calculated and paid. If you understand these rules, you can find legal ways to minimize your tax burden and save money. There are several deductions and tax credits available that many people are unaware of. That's why it's important to have an accountant or a tax expert who can guide you through these issues. Additionally, learning about investments and how the financial market works can help you make informed decisions and earn better returns. It is important to educate yourself about finances and stay up to date with changes in the system so that you can make the most of the opportunities available.

These are just a few of the strategies I've adopted on my journey towards financial freedom. Each person is unique, and their circumstances may be different, so it's important to tailor these strategies to your own needs and goals. The main thing is to change your mindset towards money and take a more conscious and responsible approach to managing your finances. With planning, discipline, and patience, you can achieve financial freedom and live a life of prosperity and generosity. Remember, wealth is not an end but a tool to achieve your dreams and help others along the way.

May God bless you on your journey, and may you find the peace and prosperity you desire.

17. There Is No "I" in Balance

There is an interesting pattern in the creation account in Genesis. At the end of each day, except for the second day, God takes account of his work and declares it good. This pattern is abruptly broken when He saw Adam alone. He said,

"It is not good for the man to be alone. I will make him a suitable helper." Genesis 2:18 (NIV)

The word Tov, good in Hebrew, directly relates to functionality. Everything God had created up to this point was fully functional according to the purpose it was created. That is how goodness is defined by God. For that reason, God created Eve from Adam's rib and placed her by his side. She provides Adam with an opposing view of reality. The phrase Ezer Neged, helper before him in Hebrew, literally means one who gives relief and support in his face (in opposition to his way of thinking by being straightforward). For Adam to function, he needs someone who will call him out by being sincere and offering support with his well-being in mind. That is exactly what we should look for in our relationships. People who see things we do not, warn us about them because they love us and want us to succeed.

Just like Adam, we quickly realize that we cannot accomplish much on our own, and even if we do, it's not as rewarding. As you progress through your journey, you will become very aware that the previously mentioned limitations will become greater. You won't have as much energy, time, or money. These resources can only be stretched so far. Even with multitasking, combining efforts, and using tools and apps to become more efficient, you'll eventually need help. You'll have to concede that it's not feasible to do everything by your-self.

Listed below are some lessons I've learned along the way. Most of them are simple truths and common sense. Still, being reminded of them tends to help us apply them more easily:

Find support: Don't be afraid to seek help or share your burdens with those around you. Find people you trust to share your frustrations and to pray for you and with you. They are all around you; you just need to ask for help. Sometimes, it is necessary to just vent or talk when you're frustrated. Just remember to be there for them when they need you.

Find mentors: Find people to look up to, those who have already achieved the goals you are pursuing and can guide you. You can avoid many pitfalls by talking to those who have reached the destination you are trying to reach.

Find counselors: This is different from mentors. These are people you have a long-term relationship with and trust to help you make difficult decisions. They may not have insights into your goal, but they have proven wisdom from the past and can help you see things from different perspectives. Remember that the final decision is yours, and they are only offering advice.

Find people who hold you accountable: These are people who face the same temptations or problems as you and can help you when you are feeling weak or overwhelmed. Because they understand what you're up against, they can offer relevant ways to avoid mistakes. Often, these people may need you as much as you need them. You can help each other in times of despair. This type of support is very common and especially helpful when trying to overcome any type of addiction.

Find people you can mentor: This is the opposite of having a mentor. Being a mentor is equally beneficial. This reinforces the knowledge you've already gained and is a way to give back. It also reminds you of how far you've come and strengthens your resolve as you take on new challenges.

Delegate responsibilities: This applies to co-workers or family members. Great leaders always delegate. If you're in charge of a team and feel tempted to do everything yourself, then you need to consciously exercise this skill. To delegate, you need to rely on someone else to do what needs to be done, and that frees you up to do other, perhaps more important, things that no one else can do.

It is something I had to put into practice myself. I had to learn to delegate some responsibilities to my daughter, which was extremely hard for me. I was used to doing everything for her throughout the years. I quickly realized that if I didn't change this, then I wouldn't be able to achieve all of our family goals. In the end, I saw that doing this was beneficial for both of us. She began to feel more useful and enjoy her responsibilities. Simultaneously, I gained time to perform other duties that she couldn't. Note: You'd be surprised how much children can accomplish if you explain the tasks to them and set some guiding rules. Part of the parental duty is getting our children ready for the world by gradually increasing their own responsibility. I can testify that today, we're both happier for it.

A sad reality is that due to modernity, many have lost their sense of community. The internet has helped us have access to knowledge easily and quickly, but it has also made us disconnected from each other. Most relationships today are virtual. We get "likes" and affirmations from total strangers and brag about how many "friends" we have on Facebook. Worst yet, anonymity has facilitated the ease of manifesting our worst selves, creating an avatar version of people who insult and destroy each other without consequences. This is making us less human in many ways. We must regain that connection with each other that I experienced growing up. Relearn to communicate face to face and build actual relationships outside the digital world. This is the main lesson in this chapter: accepting that we are all connected and need each other. There is no "I" in balance.

If you allow your personal goals to benefit those around you by sharing your vision, then you will inevitably affect them as well. Before you know it, people around you will also start to change and improve their lives. If intentionally spread, positivity and success become highly contagious.

Fact: Your personal goals can and likely will affect other people. However, you still need to pursue them for yourself.

Let me clarify that by saying this: Other people won't be enough motivation to drive you towards your goal. At least not long term.

Here is why I honestly believe this. No matter how hard you try, you cannot make others happy; each person is responsible for their own happiness. Many err on both sides of this truth. On the one hand, they seek to make others happy based on assumptions of what they want or need. In comparison, some will try to find joy from being loved or accepted by others. Neither of these paths is achievable and ends in defeat for all parties involved. Focus on becoming a better version of yourself, and the rest will fall into place. Seek out like-minded people, and you'll enrich each other's lives.

This was a short but important chapter because without it, achieving a balanced life is nearly impossible. Part of the healthy emotional aspect of our lives is closely linked to positive relationships with those around us. No one can find true and fulfilling happiness alone.

18. In the Beginning...

In the next few chapters I will share the original story I had intended to tell. The somewhat chronological testimony of events. This is the story before it evolved from a brainstorming session of memories to a book of practical lessons that can be applied by anyone. It was intended as a way to share my testimony of healing by recalling events from my traumatic experiences. A story of woes that would culminate in the exciting conclusion of God's ultimate power and sovereign healing touch. Thankfully, I was directed to focus on a more positive outlook where I could share critical lessons that happened after the healing. The final work is by no means a formula that guarantees success. It only serves as a guideline of practical truths and known tools that many already use. It can and should be modified to fit your personal needs.

When I first began sharing these notes with my sister Cynthia, she repeatedly expressed this as she read them,

— "Wow! The miracle is not just what God has done; The true miracle is how much your life was transformed after the healing."

Eventually, I agreed with her and began reorganizing my notes. The results were the chapters I have previously shared with you.

Below, I want to now give you the somewhat chronological story I lived from the day of the surgery to the day of my healing. Here is that full testimony, as I recall to the best of my ability… in graphic detail. Where it all began…

It was July 28th, 2011, a morning I remember very clearly. My mind wandered as I stared up at the ceiling, the fluorescent lights flashing faster and faster as I was wheeled down the long corridor toward the operating room. The distinct odor of iodophor, a commonly used disinfectant in hospitals, filled the atmosphere. Serving as a constant reminder of where I was and what was about to take place. I felt terrified like most people would before any serious medical procedure, but at the same time, apathetic. My conscious mind had surrendered to my fate. These mixed feelings and perceptions were a result of the pre-operation medication I was given in the prep room. It felt surreal at times. As if I was an observer outside my own body, witnessing someone else's life.

They pushed me into a cold, sterile area, and I was transferred from the gurney to a stainless-steel table. To my surprise, now I felt a strange sense of comfort. Sophisticated medical equipment and monitors surrounded me with their characteristic beeps and noises. Other nurses and healthcare workers were present. Walking around, prepping and talking amongst themselves. If I recall correctly, there were four of them in white and blue lab coats, all wearing gloves, face shields, and masks. An oxygen mask was placed over my already numb face. Further results of the pills I was given as "something to relax" me before the surgery. After that, the last thing I remember that morning was the anesthesiologist saying,

— "Get ready for a long nap. I'm going to count from ten to zero... ten... nine... eight..."

I felt the cold, strange liquid being injected through the IV drip. Followed by a weird metallic taste in my mouth. Before he got to number 4, I blacked out.

It was supposed to be a standard, minimally invasive procedure performed through laparoscopic incisions in my stomach. Gallbladder removal is now considered a simple surgery. My mom had hers removed over two decades ago; her abdomen was cut open the old way, and she recovered without incident. As misfortune would have it, the same wasn't true for me.

I woke up at a different location in what felt to me to be a blink of an eye. I later learned that more than 4 hours had passed by. I groaned as I began to feel intense pain. The nurse heard me and gave the initial prognosis,

— "Welcome back," she smiled. "Try to relax. The surgery was a success with no complications.", she added.

She gave me some pain medication, and I was kept in the hospital for a few days. Standard recovery procedure for observation and pain management. On the fourth day, I was cleared for home treatment. Nothing out of the ordinary so far, and we were all optimistic.

The first few weeks after surgery were difficult, but there were no signs that anything had gone wrong. I was on a liquid diet restriction. Even so, I barely consumed any food or drank much water. My appetite was almost non-existent. About halfway through the third week, I was finally cleared to eat a light meal with solid foods. My wife prepared a delicious catfish fillet, one of my favorite meals, with almost no seasoning and some mashed potatoes on the side. I ate slowly, trying to enjoy every bite after having been without sustenance for so long. To be honest, I don't remember the taste very well. All I do remember was experiencing nausea after eating very little. I also noticed that I felt full unusually fast. I only took a few bites and felt like I over ate. A detail that didn't seem relevant at the time but proved to be an important clue later for gastroparesis.

A few minutes after I finished that meal, I began to feel

pain. I shrug it off as having to get used to eating solids again and took the prescribed pain medication. That night, I woke up with intense pain in my stomach. As I sat up in bed, I knew I was going to vomit. I knew it was inevitable. A sensation that was confirmed as I rushed toward the bathroom. A trip interrupted when everything I had eaten that afternoon violently came out. The contents of the fluid were the undigested residue of the catfish. It was as if I hadn't digested anything that I had eaten hours ago. None of these clues made sense at the time. Only after my diagnosis and the nature of the illness would these symptoms be obvious.

That event triggered a horrible cycle. Throwing up caused the pain to intensify. So, I took more narcotics to control the pain, which caused more nausea and vomiting. Even without consuming any food, I would vomit pints of bile. This episode went on for hours unresolved. Eventually, we decided to go back to the hospital.

When we arrived at the hospital, we were instructed to see the doctor who performed the operation. He immediately admitted me and scheduled some tests to see if anything was overlooked or may have gone wrong during the surgery. For the next 30 days, I was poked, prodded, examined, and had all sorts of known tests that were related to what I experienced. None of them gave conclusive results that would explain my symptoms. The only good news was that while I was in the hospital, I had access to intravenous pain and nausea medications at all times, so the vomiting was totally under control. That was the first of a dozen similar episodes that occurred before I was properly diagnosed. Each of them dampened my hopes of finding a solution and increased the anger and frustration I began to feel toward life. Time stretched out for what seemed like an eternity. They were undoubtedly the slowest 30 days of my life. Even now, as I try to recall what has happened, I feel as if that period were months instead of 30 days.

I should add a side note here. I can't even imagine anyone facing similar circumstances without having faith and a support system I had. My wonderful wife, friends, family, and church members all provided unbelievable support. I am eternally grateful for them and their sacrifices. I also had my beloved little princess, Isabella, who was only 2 years old at the time. Her beautiful smile and unconditional love kept me going. During my stay in the hospital, those few hours I spent with her were always the highlight of my day. When I heard her adorable voice as she approached my room, my heart was instantaneously filled with joy. I thank God for her, my wife, and everyone else, including the medical staff, who took great care of me.

About six months passed with no positive change. Every time I tried to eat solid foods, I got into the same vicious cycle, which landed me back in the hospital. The trigger was also unclear. Everything was very random. I was having multiple visits to the ER on a weekly basis. It was all stressful, frustrating, and discouraging at the same time, especially since no one knew why this was happening. There was no explanation or solution in sight.

It was around this time that the doctor suggested a "gastric emptying study." It is a stomach motility test in which the patient eats eggs that contain a radioactive isotope that can be monitored through a series of CT scan images. After eating the eggs, a series of CT scans are taken periodically to identify how much of the egg mass has passed from the stomach to the small intestine. It was a day-long ordeal. I was optimistic and hopeful that this test would provide answers. At this point, hospital visits and stays had become routine, so it didn't bother me to do another test with the potential for answers.

After 8 hours later and about 6 CT scans, I was told that the doctor would analyze the data and call us to give the results. This happened in a few days when my wife Susan and I were called to receive the terrible news. This was the conversation that changed my life:

— "Mr. Santos, please sit down. Based on the test results, we know what's wrong with you." His facial expression or tone didn't convey that I was about to receive good news, but I chose to cling to my optimism.

— "The emptying test showed that after 8 hours, only 12 percent of the eggs had passed from the stomach. On a normal stomach, it would have been 100% eliminated. In fact, it should have been 100% after 4 hours."

— "So... What does that mean?" I asked in a perplexed tone.

— "It means you have severe gastroparesis," he replied reluctantly. "Your stomach isn't working properly." He added as he noted my blank stare and lack of words.

— "Great... At least we know what's wrong with me. Thank God. So, what's the treatment? What do we do now, doctor?" I questioned, with a smile, always hopeful.

— "I'm sorry to say there's no treatment or way to fix this. We can provide you with medication to help, and you will need to follow a very strict and limited diet. That's the best we can do for now." He said this as only doctors can deliver bad news. "We live in interesting times and there are some treatments being developed, but they are not yet approved by the FDA and are in the clinical trials phase. I'm sure there will be something soon. You're young," he said in a firm but monotone voice.

I know he added that last part to provide me with hope,

and the truth is that we still didn't grasp the seriousness of what we heard. We were unaware of this disease or what was involved. Something that would change very soon.

I can summarize the horrendous details of this long process that we were about to begin. To simplify, I will divide it into phases, which lasted between 1 to 3 years each (approximately). I will spare you the horrid daily details while still allowing you to see a glimpse of the magnitude of the nightmare we endured. I say we because my wife didn't experience the pain in her flesh, but she was by my side the entire time and experienced different challenges. Some that I'm familiar with now as I watch her battle cancer.

Trust me when I say that I'm not trying to be overdramatic here. It was a constant torment that extended for each agonizing day. Think of the worst cold you've ever had, add chronic pain at a level that would make you cry, and then make that your daily experience for 8 years. Make no mistake, this disease, in its mildest state, is literally hell on Earth.

Just to put it in perspective, I faced this disease for just over 8 years, which equates to approximately 3,000 days. About 95% of those days, I had constant nausea. Days that I also suffered either severe constipation or extreme diarrhea. That's about 2,700 days of waking up with extreme nausea and some other stomach discomfort. At least 80% of those days, I vomited at least once. That's 2,400 days with vomiting out of the 2,700. At least 70% of those days, I threw up several times. About 50% of those days, I threw up 10 times or more. Finally, on at least 25% of those days, I threw up more than 20 times a day, and most of them ended up in the ER.

Let me make this more clear. At least half of the days in the past 8 years, I threw up 10 or more times. Days I consider completely lost because I couldn't get out of bed except to vomit. Every time, feeling weaker and weaker as the pain intensified. That's about 1,500 days of incessant pain and vomiting, and the disease doesn't care if it's 2 in the morning. I went many days without sleeping when this cycle was triggered. There have been occasions when I have gone almost a week without sleeping a full night. I recall hallucinating before passing out from exhaustion. A respite that would only last a few precious minutes before I would wake up with my stomach filled with bile again. To put this into perspective, I was told to keep a record of everything I ate or tried to eat to identify a pattern of what triggered the cycle. On one occasion, I recorded in that diary that I threw up 54 times in one day. It doesn't even seem possible, but during the worst crises, my body produced so much bile that my stomach would fill up every 15 minutes. This would happen regardless of if I ate or drank anything.

In addition to the pain, I also had the displeasure of feeling my esophagus and mouth burn due to the bile acid my body was producing. The bile was damaging my esophagus, mouth, gums, and teeth. I often became dehydrated and had to be admitted to the hospital for fluids to replenish calories and minerals intravenously. Because my digestive system was dysregulated and because I was forced to take excessive amounts of narcotics for pain, I often suffered from constipation. This caused another problem over time. Narcotics relieved pain but slowed digestive transit and gastric motility even more. It also caused my body to gain a dependency on the drugs. Even on the best days, when I didn't need as much medication, I went into withdrawal, which caused me severe diarrhea, chills, and the consequent pain. Finding the balance was nearly impossible. So, even on good days, I had different struggles.

All these were physical symptoms and difficulties. I haven't even begun to mention the emotional and psychological damage I suffered during that period of my life. I will address these aspects in more detail as I discuss each phase. I can address them chronologically as the illness progressed. I can tell you this: the pain was so severe that sometimes I would fall to the ground and stay in the fetal position for hours, waiting and hoping for the medicine to take effect. As an adult man, I confess that, before this disease, I never cried because of pain. The pain I experienced during this period of my life led me to cry several times more often than I care to admit.

19. The Early Years

Phase 1: I'm going to call this the discovery phase and estimate that it lasted approximately a year. With newfound hope acquired by the knowledge of what was causing my distress, Susan and I began our research. We scoured the web to see what gastroparesis was and how to treat it. The internet is truly a marvel and provides easy access to information for those who seek it. Even with all the misinformation out there, if you look in the right places, you can get a lot of advice that would have been inaccessible before. We made sure to only research medical data from reliable sources such as hospitals or reputable websites. Still, we soon understood that the amount of information we found was insufficient.

We could better define the potential causes of the disease, but that didn't help us much on a day-to-day basis. Gastroparesis derives from the Greek words γαστήρ "gastro," which means stomach, and πάρεσις "paresis," which means partial paralysis. In layman's terms, it simply means a paralyzed stomach. For simplicity and to avoid mentioning this word excessively, I will refer to gastroparesis as most of us patients do: GP. Just like any type of paralysis, the cause is nerve damage, with the reasons most commonly listed being diabetes, nerve damage during surgery, viral infections, or other neurological and idiopathic diseases, i.e., unknown causes. In my instance, it was clearly caused by nerve damage during surgery.

In addition to the web searches, I joined a Facebook support group that had other patients who suffered from this disease. They were sympathetic and could share their experiences with us so that we could try to adapt to this new lifestyle.

Useful information was scarce, and the suggestions offered in the group were conflicting. We quickly recognized that everyone's body is different and, therefore, reacted randomly to any solution applied. That first year was very difficult, perhaps the hardest of all the remaining time. Each question we thought we had answered led to more unsolved mysteries. Every clue to a possible solution ended up as a dead-end. The phrase,

— "We just don't know enough about this disease."

became the echoing response we heard from every specialist and doctor we visited.

Meanwhile, the symptoms never went away or subsided. I was going to the emergency room 2 to 3 times a week and being admitted to the hospital at least once a month. Due to the nature of my illness, which involved constant vomiting, any medication I took orally would end up in the toilet, and the only way to stop the vomiting cycle was to be given intravenous medication. This resulted in constant emergency room visits, which meant endless hours in waiting rooms before we were seen, all while continuing to vomit every 15 minutes. Just thinking about it as I write brings tears to my eyes. I don't wish that on anyone.

To make matters worse, I had to endure the humiliation of being treated like a drug addict. The medical staff, for the most part, due to ignorance about GP, treated me like someone who was acting that way just to get the next fix. This seemed absurd to me because I had enough legally obtained narcotics at the house to knock out an elephant. Unfortunately, that didn't change how they dealt with me. I was treated very badly by the nurses and doctors at the ER. I know this is not something I experienced alone since I hear similar complaints from my fellow GP warriors in the Facebook support group. They all go through this indifference from health professionals. Even worse, many of them receive similar accusations from their own families. As if it were not enough to have to endure the physical pain, we also had the psychological pain of being blamed for our own suffering.

— "What did you eat this time that made you sick?"; "I told you not to try to eat that"; "It's your fault that you're sick, you keep eating things you shouldn't," are just a few choice words we heard often.

At times, they hurt more than any physical pain one might have to bear. They wound the soul.

At the end of this phase of discovery, my hopes began to slowly die, and reality set in: This is my life now, and there is no hope.

20. Making Adjustments

Phase 2: The next phase lasted about 2 years, and I would call it the adaptation phase. In this phase, I adopted many life-changing habits that helped us live with GP. Gradually, we stopped looking for a miracle cure or a definitive solution and directed our attention to improving our quality of life. My wife became an expert on all things GP, and when visiting doctors, she would make suggestions rather than ask questions. The doctors were impressed, and they often agreed and complied with her proposals. One life-changing alteration was the request to get a liquid version of the narcotic drug. It would be absorbed more quickly through the stomach wall into the bloodstream. This gave me results before vomiting, which significantly decreased the number of emergency room visits required to stop the cycles. We also kept a food diary and observed some food patterns to avoid. It wasn't an exact science, but it also helped a bit.

Still, the inevitable long-term effects began to happen. Without adequate food intake and the constant state of malnutrition, I was, like many GP patients, losing weight rapidly. Before the surgery, I was just a bit overweight for my height, 5'11", at 204lbs. Now, 18 months after the surgery, I was weighing half that. Because of this, we made an appointment to visit Ohio to see the leading researchers in this area at the Mayo Clinic to get the final recommendations from the leading experts.

Our expectations were very low after visiting numerous experts who provided us with little to no help, but we had already planned this trip and had nothing to lose. The doctor who attended us didn't have any new information, but he gave

139

us a stern warning about my weight. His suggestion was that I put in a feeding tube. I hesitated to comply since it would involve another surgery. Another reason I had to reject his recommendation was because I had not heard many positive arguments about it from other GP patients in my group. The tube clogs up often and can become infected. Not to mention that it's not very attractive. I was still willing to consider it if it helped me to improve. The doctor added,

— "Well, for now, we can hold off on my recommendation. However, if your weight drops below 100lbs, then, in my professional medical opinion, I will say it goes from suggestion to a necessity."

The only conclusion from this trip was that the situation was dire and caused us to become even more disillusioned. It was a long drive home. My latest prognosis was bleak, but we continued to fight. After all, we were given no other choice. The only possible thing we could do was to continue to try to live the best life possible in the given circumstances.

It was around this time that I began to receive home care and an effort to help me gain weight. A device was placed in my upper left arm, connected directly to my heart, where I could connect a Total Parenteral Nutrition (TPN) pump. This would provide my body with nutrients throughout the day and keep me going for a little longer while I decided if the feeding tube was right for me. TPN pumps nutrient-rich fluids into the bloodstream, bypassing the gastrointestinal tract. It is a temporary solution that cannot be administered long-term but can be helpful for about a 6-month period. My wife had to receive medical training to clean the device and change the fluids every 6 hours, and a nurse visited us once a week to monitor my progress.

I used TPN for the full allowable time. This helped quite a

bit. It improved my energy levels and even helped me increase in weight. I got up to about 120lbs, which allowed me to avoid the surgery for the feeding tube. I was so grateful for that small victory. The only downside was that this contraption attached to my body was a constant reminder of how sick I was. Everyone looked at me with either empathy or a strange curiosity. It made it obvious that something was wrong with me. It improved me physically but damaged my ego, pride and self-esteem. A trade-off that was worth it in the end, but I cannot do this testimony justice if I don't talk about its negative effects.

A helpful lesson I learned from the GP warriors on Facebook was that a long, hot shower would help with nausea, pain and stress. Managing these side effects was crucial to lowering the frequency of experienced triggers. And it was during this adaptation phase that I started using this tactic when I began vomiting. By taking long hot showers or jumping in the bathtub, I would be able to resist long enough for the liquid medication to enter the bloodstream. It didn't always work, but it helped and reduced the number of times I needed to go to the emergency room. Because of this, I started spending a lot of time in the tub. It was worthwhile, but it was extremely uncomfortable. Still, when it worked, it was a lifesaver. It certainly improved the quality of life target we were aiming for during this period.

As I continued to stabilize, I began to feel the pressure to get back to work. During these two phases, I was on short-term and eventually long-term disability through my employer, Pregis. This pressure came from a truth my wife, and I learned very quickly: creditors don't care if you're sick and the bills keep on coming. We also learned that medical insurance is useful, but has a significant number of loopholes that bleeds your savings. Words like out-of-network, deductibles, copays, personal spending, and other sneaky terms will deplete your bank account faster than anything could replenish it. In addition, both short-term and long-term sick leave were only covering a percentage of my salary. With less money coming in and a lot more going out, our savings were quickly disappearing. All this financial pressure increased another GP trigger: stress. Just as I began to stabilize one and a half years into this journey, I was about to embark on another roller coaster of instability.

My boss suggested that I gradually go back and work part-time for 3 days a week. I could then progressively increase the number of days and hours if things went well. His proposal seemed reasonable, so I decided to give it a try. Turned out that accomplishing it was much harder than I could have anticipated. Even waking up and getting ready was a huge endeavor. I would wake up 3 hours before I needed to get to the office because I had to get heavily medicated to be able to function. I had to take several pills and allow enough time for the medicine to work before I could get out of bed. Once I finally arrived at the office, I quickly became ill and had to rush back home for relief. My wife would leave the tub ready and full, awaiting my imminent arrival.

This became my new daily routine: getting ready for work, driving to work, getting sick, fighting it until it became unbearable, driving home in severe pain, spending the next 4-8 hours in the tub while taking medication and trying to control vomiting, going to sleep, only to relive this again the next morning. A routine that lasted for about 6 months. I felt as if I was living a nightmarish version of Groundhog Day (a movie from 1993 starting Bill Murry). After this trial attempt to return to work, I was let go. It simply wasn't working out, and I had reached the end of my rope. It was around this time that depression inevitably began to manifest itself. My outlook on life was hopeless, and my expectations for the future were bleak. I even contemplated ending it all. To be honest, I'm not even sure how or why I continued to try. I can only say that in those darkest moments, I felt God's love long enough to keep going. I'm very glad for His Spirit's way of conveying that message within me. If not for that, I wouldn't be writing this book today.

21. Accepting the Circumstances

Phase 3: The next phase lasted for approximately another 3 and a half years. I call it the acceptance phase. All the techniques I learned and put into practice began to slightly improve my quality of life, making the illness a bit more manageable. I find it amazing how the human spirit can adapt to the most extreme situations. During this period, I found some strength in the people who surrounded me and were fighting alongside me. I had to somehow get better for the sake of my child and family.

The symptoms of GP and its side effects never got better; I just got stronger and adapted. It was still frustrating, but I got to know my own limitations and how to avoid getting sick. I discovered what triggered the cycles and how to avoid them. I learned the right combination of prescriptions to take, depending on how I felt. I became aware of what foods I couldn't eat and avoided them at all costs. With those adjustments, I was able to get better. I still felt nauseous on a daily basis and threw up at least once most days. But at least I was no longer completely dysfunctional every day. I was able to control it before it triggered the endless vomiting cycle. It wasn't a life to be proud of, but in comparison to the previous years, it was actually an improvement. If I had to sum it up, I would say that I wasn't truly living, but at least I was surviving.

My social life was non-existent. I couldn't watch a full movie or attend a full church service on Sundays without constant interruptions. I lost count of the times I went to an event only to spend most of my time vomiting or relieving myself in the bathroom. I was completely unreliable and couldn't make any plans because I had no idea what my day-to-day life was going to be like. One of the biggest things that healthy people may not realize is how lonely a chronic illness can be. They can't possibly know without experiencing it. I didn't know this before I got GP, so I'm not judging. Life for most people is hectic and busy. Thus, it is constantly moving forward. What I learned was that for the chronically ill, it seems to completely stop. You get caught up in this never-ending sequence of events, dealing with the disease and its increasingly intense symptoms. What ends up happening is that no matter how much they care or love you, at some point, people move on. It's inevitable, and they can't be blamed. We all have our own problems to deal with. It still hurts quite a bit. You feel abandoned and see everyone's life progressing while you become a social outcast. You find yourself stuck with the unpleasant patterns that come with the disease. Social media increases this awareness exponentially. You see your friends going on trips. Starting new careers. Getting married. Celebrating holidays. As much as I wanted to share in their joy, it just made our situation seem even more hopeless. I felt angry and guilty because my situation wasn't only holding me back but affecting my wife as well.

The most positive change that occurred in this phase was that I found an excellent pain management doctor. His name is Dr. Calava. This gentleman is the embodiment of what a physician should be. He genuinely did all he could to help me get better. As I shared with him my experiences at the ER and how often I had to depend on them, Dr. Calava didn't just listen; he acted. He called the local hospital and instructed them about my condition, leaving a pre-arranged prescription for pain and nausea treatments just in case I needed to go to the emergency room for relief. I no longer had to wait hours to be seen, and when there was such a need, I didn't have to deal with rejection and ridicule before receiving much-needed medications. The staff at my local hospital knew that I wasn't just faking and understood why I needed the intravenous delivery of the medicine. He also prescribed me a pain reliever patch so I could better manage the continuous pain from the chronic illness and only have to take medication orally when absolutely necessary. The combination of this delivery system and the liquid narcotic made a noticeable difference in preventing the cycles that led me to the hospital.

With fewer frequent visits to the emergency room and these improvements, I was able to adjust to a better routine. I was even able to get a new job and function enough to maintain it. Sure, there were constant struggles. I was taking so much medication that I would fall apart without it. A combination of 3 different opioids for pain, benzodiazepines for anxiety, SSRIs for depression, 3 types of nausea medication, and motility drugs for GP. I had to take 35 different pills a day just to function. Yet, I had to admit that I was better than before.

I had accepted this sad reality as my new lot in life. I wanted to be grateful for the improvement, but to be honest, I wanted it all to be over. I still felt completely unsatisfied. Just going through the motions to provide for my daughter and wife as best as I could. I wished for death all the time. Maybe it was a side effect of the medications because I had never been suicidal before or since. Whatever it was, the solution was a complete emotional shutdown and moving forward mechanically. Taking things one day at a time.

By the end of this phase, I was in a deep depression, and every aspect of my life was destroyed. My house was foreclosed, our savings were depleted, and to make things worse, Susan was diagnosed with bone marrow cancer. I find it amazing that, given the circumstances, I called this the "adaptation" phase. Believe it or not, the first year and a half were significantly worse than what I described above.

22. God Still Performs Miracles

Phase 4: The Cure. Things got worse before they got better. This last phase lasted about a year, and some details of what happened have already been discussed in the previous chapters of this book. Most of it was positive and miraculous. I want to focus here on the first few months and how I was touched by the Lord. How He, and He alone, deserves all the credit and glory for the transformation of my life. Still, He used people and required our participation to solve the problems I faced. It is almost impossible to fully comprehend situations while you are immersed in the experience. Hindsight, as they say, is 20/20.

The truth is that we often read the Bible without taking account of how much time passes between verses. We casually read about how Jacob worked 14 years for an unrighteous master, his future father-in-law, to win Rebekah's hand in marriage. We read how Joseph was sold into slavery by his brothers and was later imprisoned for an unjust accusation by Potiphar's wife without thinking about the 13 years that passed between these events and his ascent to one of the most powerful men in the world. We read about the immediate healing of the woman who was hemorrhaging blood for 12 long years without understanding what she endured during that time. The truth is that the suffering of others can seem brief when it is not experienced personally. Those 8 years in my life were extremely painful and caused so much emotional, psychological, and physical damage that no description in this book could do it justice (not from lack of trying.) Only personal experience would allow you to fully grasp it. The very reason I hope no one comes to understand it. The only reason I went through the length of providing so much detail was in hopes that if you are facing something similar, you can find hope. So that if you experienced something similar you may be able to relate and thus glorify God. It was all to set the scene so that you could hopefully see the grandeur of the miracle.

Time is a funny thing. When you're having fun, it seems fleeting and passes so quickly, but when you're suffering agonizing pain, the minutes seem to stretch. I spent many nights on the floor, curled up in the fetal position, begging the Lord to take me out of that horrible existence. I have experienced the kind of pain that brings tears to my eyes. I'm talking about the type of crying because the body has no other way to express what it is feeling. It was the type of pain that would make your body shut down in self-defense. I would just faint. It was on one of those occasions that I had nothing left in me, and I cried out to God. In His mercy, this was also when He intervened.

I don't remember the exact date this happened, but I am certain this was the day I received healing. The healing itself happened immediately, but the improvements became evident very gradually. That night, I was crying in the shower, and I began to pray only in my thoughts.

— "Lord, I surrender my life to you. If this is your will for my life, I will continue to serve you to the best of my ability. Even if I never get better, I will serve you until I have nothing left in me. I believe you can heal. I have faith, but even if you don't, I will be grateful and live for you. I'm grateful for what Christ has already done for me. It is already more than I deserve. So, thank you."

It was a sincere prayer of surrender. I truly meant it. And it was at that time that I felt something different. A burning sensation throughout my body followed by a sudden peace and well-being. Even the pain was gone. I didn't hear anything. I didn't have visions or revelations. I just felt something I never felt before.

The next morning, my symptoms weren't as strong. My usual routine always included waking up with severe nausea, but that morning, I felt none. My first reaction was to think it was a coincidence as I had other brief periods of relief in my 8-year dealing with GP. I feared giving into hope or having any expectations again. My mental state could not bear another disappointment. A lot had gone on when the healing stage finally arrived. I was unemployed again because the contract had expired, and I was being treated by a psychiatrist to overcome the depression. Some of the details I shared earlier were already developing in this phase.

After about 3 months of therapy, I began to see improvements due to the new antidepressants and because I was following a stress management exercise. I kept experiencing minor daily improvements from that day forward. It was at this point that my therapist suggested that I should contact my family. She thought that I would benefit from additional support and that it would help me gain emotional healing. So, I called my mom for the first time in years, and we began rebuilding our relationship.

In one of our many conversations, I told her about the suspicion that God had healed me. I shared the details of the event with her and what I felt that day. I also added how gradually and steadily I had been improving day by day since the incident. It was when I told her the approximate date this all happened that she began to shout,

— "Halleluiah. Praise Jesus," her voice filled with emotion as she began to cry.

That is when she began to share something with me. Something I was completely unaware of. She said,

— "The day was October 13th, 2017. I know this based on your estimation and the time you had your experience. It was the same day that I did something very unusual myself. By faith, I prayed and confessed the sins of our past family members. I asked God to forgive and unbind any sins that we may have committed in the past."

I was shocked and skeptical. I wasn't sure what she was saying, and I immediately doubted it was even "biblical." Still, the events were undeniable, and I quickly understood that God is infinitely more incredible than we think. He can and does things as He pleases, and, as I mentioned before, He treats each person, each circumstance, and each event individually. The same Lord who healed a blind man with one touch also healed another blind man by spitting on the ground, making mud with His saliva and rubbing it on his face before ordering him to go and wash in the pool of Siloam. There are numerous accounts of Jesus healing blind people. In some cases, He healed them immediately, and in others, He gave them instructions to follow. I'm also certain that some blind men went unhealed. Not all blind people regained their sight simply because Jesus exists. I can't explain why, nor can I fully understand God's ways. The only thing I can testify is that one day I was sick and now I'm healed. Like the blind man who was told to take some actions in faith, my mother followed every step, and God honored her.

That is when I did what I always do when I'm perplexed by something. I asked her to share more so I could examine the scriptures. She shared the complete story, and I began to pray as I searched the scriptures. Her testimony is this:

She was praying and pleading with God on my behalf. The kind of prayer only a mother who loves her child can say. I can relate and only sympathize as a father. I feel a fraction of that pain as I witness my wife battling cancer and how much more

I would ache if that were my daughter. After this intense period of prayers. Days at the feet of God crying and pleading she happened to see a video on her YouTube video feed about the testimony of Pastor Tania Teresa. The video caught her eye, and she decided to watch it. The video gave her own testimony of healing and how God showed her the legalism of the spiritual realm. Pastor Tania was also a retired judge, and she understood the world through the legal system. In her knowledge and research, God revealed to her how He, as a Righteous Judge, MUST follow His own laws. My mom was hooked. She watched several videos from Tania and eventually believed. On that night, October 13th, my mom simply followed the instructions by faith. She acted on her faith.

After watching the same videos and researching her thought process by examining the scriptures, I also became a believer in what she was teaching. Simply because her teachings were grounded in the scriptures. So much that some of her teachings I put into practice and influenced many ideas I shared in this book. Of course, I cannot give you the details of all she teaches here in my book. Her teachings also span several books that she has authored. She currently has written 18 books (some available in English) explaining many principles in detail, as well as countless testimonies of how people's lives have been touched by following them.

I encourage anyone to get this literature and do their own research. The only available title in English is called "Breaking Paradigms About Spiritual Inheritances," which is the main book where her ministry began.

The main takeaway from this is that **"faith without works is dead" James 2:20b (NIV)**. The book of James is so often misunderstood. Its central message is that a saving faith acts. Once you believe, you need to apply it. That is what my mom did. She believed the message and believed that for God, nothing is impossible. I can proudly boast that I had done nothing to deserve or earn this wonderful gift. Absolutely nothing. In fact, I had given up. If it were up to me, I'd still be sick or maybe dead. It was all God, from beginning to end, and He used Pastor Tania and my mom as vessels to help me overcome this trial. For that, I am eternally grateful.

If you are in a similar situation, I advise you to research and experience the same victory in your life. If the problem that affects you is spiritual, there is nothing physical you can do to overcome it. Perhaps something physical can help make the problem more tolerable. But if the problem comes from things of the past and is linked to spiritual heritages, the solution is to detach yourself from these "contracts" through confession. All of these concepts are biblical and clearly explained in the Bible. Pastor Tania has been instructed in this area and its efficacy speaks for themselves. She often says this,

— "Against facts, there are no arguments" in her YouTube lectures. Another thing she says very often is,

— "God has shown me these truths through experience. I have no power to do anything. I simply follow His instructions, and things happen. It's undeniable."

If you wish, you can search for her on all social media platforms by her full name Tania Teresa. Most of her videos have been translated or have English subtitles.

The rest of my story has already been shared. I started the book at the end of my journey. I presented my story in a flashback movie style, mostly because I wanted to focus on the positive first. My testimony is a bit morbid if presented otherwise. The only purpose of sharing it was to encourage you and hopefully enrich your life. It was important to share what I experienced, as dark as it was, so you could see that no matter what you are facing right now, God has a way out. There is always hope with Him.

My intention is not to shove God's message down your throat. I have no ulterior motive. I'm not trying to gain your sympathy to recruit you into any church or belief system. I'm not trying to get you to invest or give me money. Still, it would be an injustice for me to testify about God's greatness and how He has changed my life without also letting you know that He loves you personally and wants to do the same for you. My journey has been difficult, but as I look back, I can say that God has never abandoned me, and I have learned valuable lessons along the way. I am much stronger, and I have overcome obstacles I never thought possible with His help.

For all these reasons and more, I believe the last chapter is the most important. Please read it carefully and with an open heart.

23. Receive Shalom

My entire book has been presenting you with ways that you can receive the fullness of life through Christ. If it wasn't obvious enough, this premise implies that in order to receive that fullness, you need to first believe in the One who offers it. Without Christ, there is no Shalom. So understandably you need to first surrender your life to Him. This is a long chapter filled with deep truths that you will need to digest. Read it slowly and with care. The concepts, just like in my book, build upon each other. If necessary, re-read the sections and noted scriptures in their full context until you understand. Even if you hold a different opinion on the matter, it is still important to be clear on what I'm trying to convey so you can grasp the entire message. In the end, you will make your own decision. Free will is a gift given by the Creator, so who am I to obstruct that gift? My only requirement is to express my faith providing biblical reasons why I believe it. As it is instructed in the letter from Peter to the first-century church,

"Who is going to harm you if you are eager to do good? But even if you should suffer for what is right, you are blessed. 'Do not fear their threats; do not be frightened.' But in your hearts, revere Christ as Lord. Always be prepared to give an answer to everyone who asks you to give the reason for the hope that you have. But do this with gentleness and respect" 1 Peter 3:13-15 (NIV)

I'm here to testify. The rest is not up to me. It is the work of the Spirit and your decision to heed or ignore it. Let's begin…

THE DISEASE, THE CURE AND THE ACCUSATION

I do understand that no sane person would accept a cure if they did not know they were sick. If a man came up to you on the street and said,

— "Hey, buddy, I've come to tell you that you need this medication if you want to survive. Just take this pill and live. If you don't, you'll die in a few weeks."

You and most reasonable people would probably look at him and think,

— "Who is this guy? I don't know him. Why should you trust him? He might be giving me poison." and likely walk away.

An inquisitive person may even ask a few questions before dismissing that person as crazy and walking away. Those who have encountered some crazy people in the past may even use a few choice words in anger before they leave. This is exactly how most people respond to the Gospel today. It is unfortunate, but the church has often been guilty of improperly presenting the most wonderful story ever told.

The word "Gospel" means "good news." The good news is this: You can be saved if you trust Jesus Christ as your Savior. Through that salvation, you can also achieve balance and live a fruitful life. However, just like the pill offered by the stranger, a logical response would be:

— "Save me from what? I don't need salvation."

An alternate analogy would be that people reject punishment without knowledge of having broken a rule or committed a crime. Most people's reaction to being pulled over by a cop is to question what they did wrong. Especially if they weren't doing something obviously wrong. I remember one time a friend of mine was pulled over by a police officer and immediately started yelling at him in a disrespectful tone,

155

— "I know I wasn't speeding... What did you stop me for?"

— "Ma'am, I stopped you because you have a broken taillight. Can I see your driver's license and vehicle registration, please?" the policeman replied monotonously.

Her attitude immediately changed. She wasn't aware of the broken taillight but now realized that he had just cause to stop her.

And that, in short, is how most people reject the Gospel today. They have no reference to God's true message or why He sent His Son. The messenger and the message have become so disconnected from the audience that, unless they are explained, they lose their impact. Before you can receive the Gospel, there are a few concepts you need to understand. Many people may come to this understanding in different ways, but they all come by the same path: the Holy Spirit. The Bible says,

"No one can say, 'Jesus is Lord,' except by the Holy Spirit" 1 Corinthians 12:3b (NIV)

Therefore, my continual and fervent prayer as I wrote these words was that the Spirit of God will speak to you as you read them. I will present God's plan in a completely logical way, but your acceptance will be the result of humility and sensitivity to the Spirit. God will not subvert your free will. The final choice is yours alone. My job is to present you with the facts in a logical way. Contrary to what most people think, faith in God is not devoid of logic.

Myth: To believe in God, you must put logic aside.

Hence, let's continue. Based on my arguments so far, before I present the good news, I must first give you the bad. Otherwise, you will reject the cure, and you won't accept responsibility for this accusation. In simple terms and without beating around the bush, the bad news is this: We have all sinned and are all guilty before a holy God. Without reconciliation, the scriptures define our destination. It is called the second death (eternal separation from God or the death of the soul). We will all die physically, but what most people fail to understand is that we will also potentially die again. The death of the soul. Here's why…

THE LAW, LOVE, AND JUSTICE

God's established laws exist, regardless of whether we are aware of them or not. Just as manmade laws we may be unaware of also exist and are upheld. Law enforcers don't care about feelings or excuses when they are being administered. That is, they don't discriminate when they are following established laws. Justice, as they say, is indeed blind. As I've shared these concepts over the years, I've heard all sorts of protests. Some of them were echoed by me when I didn't fully understand the severity of these statements. So, I'll give you logical responses to each of them. Track with me because this, as previously stated, in my opinion, is the most important discussion you will have in your life. It may affect the most important decision you may ever make. For those reasons, I will not rush these explanations because they are that important. In order to lay your doubts to rest I will answer them in a logical, but also simple way. The same way I have explained them to my child (again, not being condescending here, just making sure readers of every level understand). Nothing is based on special or new revelations. All these concepts are clearly stated in scriptures for those who seek them out.

Let's start by defining a few words. I'm assuming you already know them, as they are commonly used, but I need to ensure they are understood within this context:

1. **Injustice**: Occurs when the absence of just consequences is applied when a law is broken.
2. **Justice**: Occurs when a law is broken, and consequences are applied to correct or minimize the harm done to the victim.
3. **Mercy**: Occurs when a law is broken, guilt is acknowledged, but the consequences are not enforced by the authorities because a pardon is given by the offended party.
4. **Grace**: Occurs when a law is broken, guilt is acknowledged, but not only are consequences not applied, but additional remedies are offered by the offended party.

Here is my own little parable with practical examples used to explain these words to my little girl:

Let's say someone steals $10 from my wallet and never gets caught. That would be an injustice against me.

Now, imagine this same scenario. However, the offender is caught red-handed, and I call the police. The money is immediately returned to me, and they arrest the criminal. That's justice.

Next, if the same scenario occurs, but when the perpetrator is caught, he apologizes to me and pleads for mercy. He tells me that he desperately needed the money to prevent his family from starving. I feel the sincerity in his voice and sympathize with his situation. Because of this, I chose to forgive him and not call the cops. That's mercy.

Lastly, I feel so deeply moved by his story that I not only chose not to call the cops but also offered to help him. That's grace. When grace is applied, the victim not only absolves the penalty for the crime but also offers the criminal something more.

Please understand that in every scenario, regardless of the thief's motive, he is morally responsible. Justification or feelings don't alter the fact that he committed a crime. Even if the reason can influence how he is treated by the victim or the authorities, the acknowledgment that a crime was committed is recognized by both parties.

In the same perspective, the God of the Bible is just. He is often described as a Righteous Judge. As such, He cannot go against His own laws. As the Judge of the universe, He chose to pay for the loss and offer us grace (not just forgiveness but a full life). That is what Christ accomplished on that cross. He paid the penalty in full and now offers us something more.

A common objection to this is: If God is love, why doesn't He just choose to forgive us? Unfortunately, that is just not how the law works. He is love, but His love coexists with justice, and He cannot be only loving or only just. There are many parties involved, and if He were only loving, justice would never prevail. For instance, if someone killed your son and the judge, out of love, released the murderer, you would never receive justice. The judge's act of love toward the murderer would not be loving toward you, and the decision would certainly not be fair.

God should be held to His own standards, or He ceases to be truthful and, therefore, ceases to be God. Through Jesus, God has made a way to fully satisfy His justice while still being graceful to us.

The next common objection is this: God is being unfair by making me face the consequences for my mistakes, saying,

— "Everyone does this, so why should I be punished?"

This is another fallacy on our part. Here's a real-life example of what happened in my youth:

I was young, foolish, and thought I owned the truth. One day I was driving when I was pulled over for speeding. The policeman approached the car, and I said sarcastically:

— "Officer, I know I was speeding, but I was going at the same speed as everyone else. If you issue me a ticket, you'll have to do the same for everyone else."

— "Yes, they were all breaking the law, and if I could stop them all, I would, but since that's not possible, you won that lottery. It would be ideal to fine everyone; however, I'll have to console myself in giving it only to you. The fact that everyone else broke the law is no excuse to do the same," he replied.

I learned some hard lessons that day. As I drove home with a substantial fine on the passenger seat, I learned that using other people's guilt does not absolve my misconduct. In the same way, we need to understand that we will be judged individually, not collectively. God will not judge us on a curve. We will not be compared to other people's behavior. Our standard will be God himself on the Day of Judgment.

GOD'S STANDARD FOR JUDGMENT

This helps me segue to another common misconception: We think we're good people. Ask anyone if they think they're a good person, and I guarantee that at least 80% will answer "yes." We do this because our standards are based on comparison to others. We judge ourselves based on serial killers and people like Hitler or Stalin. If they were the standard, then we would absolutely be good. However, God's definition of good is a perfect moral standard. It is a definition so widely accepted that as a noun, the Oxford dictionary defines it as righteousness.

This sense of self-righteousness is amplified by our human nature. We tend to overlook our own faults while magnifying the mistakes of others. This victim mentality is even more prevalent these days. However, this is clearly not God's standard of goodness nor how He judges our actions.

If we admit that, in fact, we are not good by His standards, then the next common objection is:

— "God made me this way, so how can He judge me?"

This is called blame-shifting. A tactic that didn't work out too well for Adam or Eve. When confronted by God, they tried this blame-shifting strategy. In the end they received the just punishment for their individual actions. I completely relate to this objection. After all, we adopted a fallen world with fallen creatures and the consequences of a whole lot of sins we didn't commit. Yet, we are still in full control of how we react. We can't choose where we're born, who our parents are, our color, race, gender, and a myriad of other innate characteristics. Still, none of that is a valid excuse for how we choose to live our lives. The cards we've been dealt don't dictate how we play them, and we're expected to do the best we can with what we've been given. The perpetual lie that many will dish out as a result of these variables is that God loves you just as you are. The truth is that God loves you enough to not want you to remain as you are. I don't mean your appearance or your personality. He desires to change your circumstances and life if you allow Him to do so. He doesn't want clones and everyone to be the same, but He does want everyone to be righteous.

I know a lot of you will be turned off by this, but I truly believe this is a fact. I believe there are enough scriptures and evidence to back this up. The Lord did not create evil and opposes it. His very nature is evidence of this.

Myth: Good cannot exist without evil, so God created evil for a purpose.

Almost all religions or representations of God in the secular view have this dualistic nature in mind. Yin and Yang are a perfect example. One side is bad, but it has a little bit of good in it, and the other side is good, with a little bit of evil in it. However, the God of the Bible is not dualistic in His nature. The Bible states that **"God is light; in him, there is no darkness at all." 1 John 1:5 (NIV).** It also says, **"When tempted, no one should say, 'God is tempting me.' For God cannot be tempted by evil, nor does he tempt anyone." James 1:13 (NIV),** and **"Every good and perfect gift is from above, coming down from the Father of the heavenly lights, who does not change like shifting shadows." James 1:17 (NIV).** The God of the Bible, the one true Creator God, has no darkness and detests evil. He is holy. Set apart from any other entity. He is unique and different. He may use negative situations for the good of His loved ones, but He has not caused or desired evil things to happen to you. I say all this because I believe that however God judges in the end, it will be just, and no one will miss out on an opportunity to know what is good and bad. Romans 2 explains this in detail. Even if you have never heard God's laws or about any of this, the scriptures state the following:

"God will repay each person according to what they have done. To those who, by persistence in doing good, seek glory, honor and immortality, he will give eternal life. But for those who are self-seeking and who reject the truth and follow evil, there will be wrath and anger. There will be trouble and distress for every human being who does evil: first for the Jew, then for the Gentile; but glory, honor and peace for everyone who does good: first for the Jew, then for the Gentile. For God does not show favoritism. All who sin apart from the law will also perish apart from the law, and all who sin under the law will be judged by the law. For it is not those who hear the law who are righteous in God's sight, but it is those who obey the law who will be declared righteous. Indeed, when Gentiles,

who do not have the law, do by nature things required by the law, they are a law for themselves, even though they do not have the law. They show that the requirements of the law are written on their hearts, their consciences also bearing witness, and their thoughts sometimes accusing them and at other times even defending them. This will take place on the day when God judges people's secrets through Jesus Christ, as the gospel declares." Romans 2:6-16 (NIV)

THE VERDICT

I hope a clear picture of impending doom is beginning to form in your mind. If not, let me reiterate some facts that will make you contemplate and understand your position before a holy and just God (all our positions without a Savior):

> 1. God has established moral and spiritual laws.
> 2. We have all violated at least one of His laws. Likely to have done it countless times. (Think of how many lies you have told in your life).
> 3. One day, we will stand before Him to give an account of our actions.
> 4. God is righteous and, therefore, follows His own laws. He is impartial and doesn't offer favoritism.

Based on these facts, we can begin to see why we need a Savior. If you are still not convinced, allow me to present some additional evidence to the "court." Let's say you're before a judge for committing a crime. For the sake of argument, let's say you've been caught and charged with possession of illegal substances. As you appear before the judge, you are allowed to present a defense. I can assure you of one thing: the judge in charge, whoever he may be, will not accept this argument as a defense:

— "Hello, your honor. I am aware that I have been caught with an illegal substance and that it is against the law, but I have done a lot of good things throughout my life, and this was the only time I made a mistake. I go to church, give to the poor, and volunteer my time every week. Therefore, I should be pardoned for the drug possession charge since I've done more good than evil. Thank you for your consideration."

Again, that's just not how the law works. Good deeds do not erase bad ones. Even if a person has lived a perfect life up to that point, once he kills someone and becomes a murderer, he will be judged for his crime. The judge will not look at the good versus bad and then rule in your favor. A good and just judge will simply follow the law.

Ignorance of the law will also not excuse you. If you chose a different defense by stating that you didn't even know that substance was illegal, the judgment against you will not change.

Laws and those responsible for upholding them must be impartial. Otherwise, the system is broken. We are used to our manmade legal system and how it is corrupt and honestly dysfunctional, but God's court will be perfect just as His laws are. Hopefully the next logical question would be: By what laws will God judge mankind? My belief is that He will judge us based on His moral laws. The ones we call the Ten Commandments. These are the laws that Romans 2 states are written in our hearts. They are mostly common laws that seem to surpass any religious dogma. These are laws that, when broken, cause our conscious immediate shame and are usually followed by a conscious that either accuses or excuses us.

Before I list them here, I would like to remind everyone, especially modern Christians, that God's moral laws still apply today. Jesus Himself said,

"Do not think that I have come to abolish the Law or the Prophets; I have not come to abolish them, but to fulfill them." Matthew 5:17 (NIV)

A sad misconception by the Christian community is to think that God is speaking about the Laws of Moses and that Christ came to eliminate our need to obey them. The Torah (the first five books of the Bible) contains about 623 laws transmitted by Moses to the Israelites. They include ceremonial, judicial, civil, and common laws. Many of them are not relevant today, and that's where the error comes from. God's moral law, the laws that He has written with His own finger on the tablets of stone, are the ones we'll be measured against. These laws were not abolished by Jesus. In fact, He made them even more rigorous by expanding and clarifying their meanings. Here they are in detail:

1st Command given through Moses in **Exodus 20:3** was **"You shall have no other gods before me"**. Jesus affirmed this in **Luke 4:8 "It is written: 'Worship the Lord your God and serve Him only."**

2nd Command given through Moses in **Exodus 20:4-6** was **"You shall not make for yourselves an image in the form or anything in the heaven above or on the earth beneath or in the waters below. You shall not bow down to them to worship or serve them.".** This is covered under **Luke 4:8** as well.

3rd Command in **Exodus 20:7** states, **"You shall not misuse the name of the Lord your God, for the Lord will not hold anyone guiltless who misuses His name"**. Jesus teaches similar with examples including **"but whoever speaks against the Holy Spirit will not be forgiven, either in this age or in the one to come" Matthew 12:32b** and **"...but I tell you not to swear at all: either by heaven, for it is God's throne..."** full context see **Matthew 5:33-37**

165

4th Command in **Exodus 20:8** was **"Remember the Sabbath day by keeping it holy"**. Jesus expanded this understanding with **Mark 2:27 "The Sabbath was made for man, not man for the Sabbath"**

5th Command in **Exodus 20:12a** states, **"Honor your father and mother..."** and Jesus teaches us to both **"honor your father and your mother"** as well as **"love your neighbor as yourself"** in **Matthew 19:19.**

6th Command in **Exodus 20:13** states, **"You shall not murder"**, but Jesus **goes beyond by exclaiming, "If you hate your brother, you have already committed murder in your heart"** in **Matthew 5:21,22**

7th Command in **Exodus 20:14** teaches, **"You shall not commit adultery"**, but Jesus again raises the bar by saying, **"If you look lustfully, you have already committed adultery in your heart"** in **Matthew 5:27,28.**

8th Command in **Exodus 20:15** says, **"You shall not steal"**. Jesus reaffirms this in **Matthew 19:18.**

9th Command in **Exodus 20:16** states, **"You shall not give false testimony against your neighbor"** and Jesus reaffirms this in **Matthew 19:18** with **"Do not bear false witness."**

Lastly, the 10th Command in **Exodus 20:17** says, **"You shall not covet your neighbor's house. You shall not covet your neighbor's wife, hi male or female servant, his ox or donkey, or anything that belongs to your neighbor."** Jesus speaks against coveting riches in many occasion. **Matthew 6:19-21** and **16:26** are just a few.

Each of these laws remains in effect. Some were just clarified by Jesus while on earth. The laws that caused the most confusion was better defined by the Lord to avoid obscurity. In fact, by doing this, Jesus made them even more rigid. Showing how seriously God deals with sin. Breaking any of these laws even once is enough to merit a just punishment. The Bible says that the payment for sin is death. Just like the wages you receive from your employer for working, the punishment for sin is earned, like a salary. Your employer doesn't give you money out of charity. If you work, you deserve your earnings. In the same way, we are storing up wrath when we break the laws He established. Storing up wrath for the Day of Judgement. A horrific thought when we understand that the punishment is the death of the soul. Every human being is currently on death row. Awaiting their turn to present their case before the Judge of all things. Jesus said this about this day,

"But I tell you that everyone will have to give account on the day of judgment for every empty word they have spoken. For by your words, you will be acquitted, and by your words you will be condemned." Matthew 12:36,37 (NIV)

What justification will you bring before the King? Before the Righteous Judge of the Universe? What is your strategy? Your defense? I cringe as I imagine some of the things I've heard come out of atheist's mouths. It will be a terrible day indeed for those who have become self-righteous. The truth is that we have no defense, and it is made evident by the scriptures:

"Now we know that whatever the law says, it says to those who are under the law, so that every mouth may be silenced and the whole world held accountable to God. Therefore no one will be justified in His sight by works of the law. For the law merely brings awareness of sin." Romans 3:19 (NIV)

And the law has been clearly established, as well as its consequences both through scripture and reality. Both dictate that every single human will die because of sin and immediately face judgment. In the book of Genesis, God warned Adam and Eve about the consequences of partaking the forbidden fruit. In His warning, He said,

"But you must not eat from the tree of the knowledge of good and evil, for when you eat from it you will certainly die." Genesis 2:17 (NIV)

A misconception here is that God was forbidding them from receiving knowledge. In fact, God's only reason for placing this knowledge within access to humanity was to test their fidelity while allowing them free will. The same courtesy extended to us today. Mankind had a choice to seek knowledge in their own way or through the Creator. The consequences were clear. Another misconception is that they didn't die. In fact, that same day, they died spiritually. Made evident by losing the light from God that clothed them when they were in their original state. From the moment they ate from the tree, they were separated from God, the source of all life. Because God is holy, and He cannot be in the presence of sin without judging it. It was only a matter of time before their physical bodies also died.

In the same way, what we call hell is simply the absence of God. A place reserved for separation from Him, the source of all that is good, until ultimate destruction (second death). If you choose to be separated from the source of life, your life will eventually cease. It's like unplugging an iPhone from the power outlet. The phone will work and last for a few hours, but it will run out of power at some point and stop working. I often say this, and it's hard to comprehend at first, but in fact, God doesn't send anyone to hell. We chose it. The Lord has provided a way through His own blood, and we can choose to receive it or reject it. God gives us free will to receive or reject His sacrifice of reconciliation. If we reject Him, He will judge us and give us what we want: a life without Him and His principles. You want to know the verdict? Here is what the Bible says,

"For God did not send His Son into the world to condemn the world, but to save the world through Him. Whoever believes in Him is not condemned, but whoever does not believe has already been condemned, because he has not believed in the name of God's one and only Son. And this is the verdict: The Light has come into the world, but men loved the darkness rather than the Light because their deeds were evil. Everyone who does evil hates the Light, and does not come into the Light for fear that his deeds will be exposed. But whoever practices the truth comes into the Light, so that it may be seen clearly that what he has done has been accomplished in God." John 3:17-21 (NIV)

THE CHOICE

The laws God established cannot be broken. Even He cannot break them and remain just. One of these laws is that without the shedding of blood, there is no remission of sin. This is how He continued to have a connection with humanity, including Adam and Eve, after they fell from their original condition. When they stood before God, naked and ashamed, the Creator covered them with animal skins. This was, in fact, the first animal sacrifice and innocent bloodshed to cover their wrongs. Animal skins were taken from dead innocent animals. However, this solution was only temporary.

For men to be fully reconciled to God, the blood of an equivalent creation had to be shed. Man for man. That is why God became a Man, lived an innocent life, and offered Himself on behalf of anyone who would receive Him as a substitutionary sacrifice for sin. You can only pay for your sin in two ways: with your own blood or with the blood of the Savior. The choice is clear, but most people reject it.

One day, the Bible says, **"every knee will bow, and every tongue will confess that Jesus Christ is Lord"** in Romans 14:11. I believe that day will be the day when we stand before the Righteous God, and He will reveal to us all the opportunities we have been given and all the mistakes we have made. We will be without excuse while standing before Him and the multitude of witnesses present. Some will bow in awe because they recognized God's greatness before the Day of Judgment, but others will be compelled to bow in humility because they refused the Savior's gesture and love. I pray that you will stand with me and with many who have chosen to believe in and receive Christ before the Judgment.

In conclusion, I ask you: how has God provided a way to love and forgive us without violating His own laws and remaining righteous without violating our free will? He paid the fine for our mistakes with His own blood. In this way, His justice can be fulfilled while also granting us mercy. A plan so sophisticated and perfect that only a majestic God could have elaborated. Simple enough for a child to understand, yet perplexing enough to confound the wise. Not in a million lifetimes will we fully comprehend the perfection of His plan.

I proudly boast about His infinite wisdom, for He has revealed His greatness to the least of us:

"For the foolishness of God is wiser than human wisdom, and the weakness of God is stronger than human strength. Brothers and sisters, think of what you were when you were called. Not many of you were wise by human standards; not many were influential; not many were of noble birth. But God chose the foolish things of the world to shame the wise; God chose the weak things of the world to shame the strong. God chose the lowly things of this world and the despised things— and the things that are not—to nullify the things that are, so that no one may boast before him. It is because of him that

you are in Christ Jesus, who has become for us wisdom from God—that is, our righteousness, holiness and redemption. Therefore, as it is written: 'Let the one who boasts boast in the Lord.'" 1 Corinthians 1:25-31 (NIV)

I pray you choose to join us in what you may consider foolishness if you feel the prompting of the Spirit, who compels and drives us toward truth.

PAID IN FULL BUT NOT APPLIED

When Christ died on the cross, He exclaimed, **"It is finished"** in **John 19:30**. The sins of the world were placed upon Him. Through His righteousness, the penalty for sin was expunged. The blood of Christ is sufficient to cover all the sins of the world, but it must be applied. After His death, free will is the only obstacle that prevents us from being reconciled to God the Father.

It begs the question, if Jesus' death and blood are sufficient to save the whole world, then why isn't everyone saved? It's not enough to just say a prayer. True Christianity is not a religion. God requires and desires a relationship with us. An alliance. A contract. Just like wedding vows, a wedding is not just about what is said on the day of the ceremony; it should be a lifelong commitment.

To enter into this contract, you must first recognize that you have indeed broken God's Laws and then repent. Repentance is a sincere desire to change your ways. It is not enough to admit your shortcomings; but you should also do your best not to remain in your error. This is the meaning of being born again. It is supernatural and happens when you have this life-changing encounter with God. It isn't a rehearsed prayer that we are prompted to say by a preacher or a fellow believer. You just need to truly mean it and speak with the

Creator in your own words. I will share my born-again experience:

When I was prompted by the Spirit, I was alone in my room in the summer of 1992. I didn't know how to pray or what words to say. I remember reading the Gospel of Jesus, as John wrote, that very day from beginning to end. When I read that Jesus was being crucified, with people spitting in His face and mocking Him, I thought,

— "That should be me. He doesn't deserve this."

I knew I wasn't good, but He was. A revelation that came to me through the Holy Spirit. I stopped reading and started sobbing like a child. I didn't have the words to express what I was feeling, but I knew it was real. The only words that came out of my mouth were,

— "Sorry, Lord," as I cried for a very long time.

As I kept repeating these words, all the bad decisions I had made came to my mind, and with each thought, I cried out again,

— "I'm sorry, Lord."

I had never killed anyone, and I was still a virgin at the time, so compared to other people, I could boast that I was a good person, but in my heart, I knew that I had offended God and broken His laws. They were His moral standards, not mine or the world's.

And that was my prayer of salvation. Four words repeated over a period of time. I'm using this example to prove that there are no magic set of words to recite. The true requirement is a genuine, repentant heart that is willing to admit guilt and accept grace by confession with your lips. It has been more than twenty years since I prayed that prayer.

I've made thousands of mistakes since then, but I always strive not to sin and to please God.

This entire book was about how to receive the fullness of life and how we can achieve a balanced life by setting and achieving goals. Finding the balance between the spiritual and the physical realms. Balance to achieve victory and obtain an abundant life. Without Christ, there is no balance. Without Christ, there is no true victory. I urge you to seek God while He can be found, and my prayer again is that the Holy Spirit will touch you and that you will not resist Him. May the Lord bless you wherever you are on this journey.

I conclude with the Words of the Most High God, through the Apostle Paul, in the letter to the Romans:

"Brethren, my heart's desire and my prayer to God for the Israelites (including the church) is that they may be saved. For I can testify that they have a zeal for God, but their zeal is not based on knowledge." Romans 10:1-2 (NIV)

"If you confess with your mouth that Jesus is Lord and believe in your heart that God raised him from the dead, you will be saved. For with the heart, one believes unto righteousness, and with the mouth, one confesses unto salvation. As the Scripture says, 'Everyone who trusts in him will never be ashamed.' There is no difference between Jew and Gentile, for the same Lord is Lord of all and richly blesses all who call upon Him because, 'Everyone who calls on the name of the Lord will be saved.'" Romans 10:9-13 (NIV)

"The Lord bless you, and keep you; the Lord make his face shine on you and be gracious to you; the Lord turn his face toward you and give you שָׁלוֹם Shalom!" Numbers 6:24-26 (NIV)

About the Author

Vancler Santos has over a decade of experience in Project Management. He has led medium to large teams on software solution implementations for multibillion dollar companies in the oil and gas industries. Recently, he has used his extensive knowledge in this field to succeed in his personal endeavors. By manipulating the tools used in project management, he was able to apply these same principles to advance his life goals. Some of which he shares in this book. Principles that can be useful to anyone in any situation.

After receiving a second chance in life through miraculous healing, his wish is to pass the knowledge he received to you, the reader. To help you be encouraged to seek the God who helped him achieve balance, to Receive Shalom.

Beyond his professional achievements, Vancler is a passionate traveler and art enthusiast dedicated to teaching and learning Hebrew. He takes immense pride in his role as a father to his daughter Isabella and cherishes his happy marriage to his wife, Susan.

Acknowledgements

I cannot, in good conscience, end this testimony without thanking my friend Douglas Huskins, who challenges my faith in a constructive way. Doug has helped me polish and flesh out some ideas with intelligent questions and pushback. He assisted me in editing and formatting the chapters in a comprehensive way. He did all this while still allowing me to express my faith and tell my story with integrity.

His insights and initial response helped me gauge how clearly my instructions came across from a believer who doesn't share my views in every aspect. It made me refine the explanations in a way that most people will hopefully comprehend.

I must also acknowledge my dear Pastor and his wonderful wife, Bruce and Janet McArthy. They, along with the rest of the congregation at Owasso First Assembly, have played a crucial role in my recovery and spiritual life before, during and after my experience with GP. They offered spiritual and financial support during this horrible ordeal. I'm so grateful for their lives and can only hope to repay them someday and somehow through service and prayer. This entire congregation is a model to many, and I'm extremely proud to be a member of this community. I can truly only describe them as family.

Speaking of family, I am obviously thankful to all my family members, but especially Enéas and Vera Muniz (my second set of parents) as well as Susane Muniz (my dear sister-in-law) for all their support during difficult times and for all the joy shared during the good times. I love you all!

www.ingramcontent.com/pod-product-compliance
Lightning Source LLC
LaVergne TN
LVHW051236080426
835513LV00016B/1621